CHRIST IS ALL SPIRITUAL MATTERS

and

THINGS

WATCHMAN NEE

Living Stream Ministry
Anaheim, California • www.lsm.org

First Edition, January 2001.

ISBN 0-7363-0355-3

Published by

Living Stream Ministry
2431 W. La Palma Ave., Anaheim, CA 92801 U.S.A.
P. O. Box 2121, Anaheim, CA 92814 U.S.A.

Printed in the United States of America

02 03 04 05 / 10 9 8 7 6 5 4 3 2

CONTENTS

INTRODUCTION

IS IT CHRIST, OR IS IT SOMETHING ELSE?

The following five chapters are messages given by the Lord's servant some time ago. Because of the present urgent need of all the saints everywhere for these kinds of messages, we have published them today.

According to God's desire, plan, and redemption, He has ordained that His Son, our Lord Jesus Christ, be all spiritual matters and things. When a man touches Him, he touches the reality of all spiritual matters and things. After a man gains Him, he gains all spiritual matters and things that God has prepared for him. But man has replaced Him with many so-called spiritual things. Although these many things, in man's eyes, belong to Him, they are nevertheless not Him. Rather, they are a replacement of Him. Therefore, they do not render man real help in his spiritual life.

We are facing a serious problem! What are we pursuing? What do we know, and what have we gained in the spiritual realm? Is it Christ, or is it something else? If it is Christ, we are touching the reality that God has ordained for us. If it is something else, no matter how good and valuable, we are merely touching vain and unprofitable things!

Today Christ is in the Spirit. In order to touch Him, we must be in spirit. We can use our mind to touch the things which are apart from Him. But in order to touch Him, we have to use the spirit. In order to touch the things that are apart from Him, we only need human zeal and cleverness. But in order to touch Him, we need God's revelation. We have to look to Him for His mercy and grace!

Witness Lee

CHAPTER ONE

CHRIST IS THE WAY,
THE TRUTH, AND THE LIFE

Scripture Reading: John 14:6

The Lord Jesus said, "I am the way, the truth, and the life" (KJV). This shows us something very clearly. What is the way that God has given us? It is Christ. What is the truth that God has given us? It is Christ. What is the life that God has given us? It is Christ. Christ is our way, Christ is our truth, and Christ is our life. Through Christ we go to the Father. In God's eyes, everything that has to do with God is Christ, who is His Son. This is why our Lord said, "I am the way, the truth, and the life; no one comes to the Father except through Me." What God has given us is just Christ; He has not given us many things apart from Christ. Many times, in spiritual matters, we see only things, and what we touch are merely things. These things are merely terms and letters to us; they do not have any spiritual value. May the Lord open our eyes so that we may know the Son of God. The characteristic of Christianity, the root of Christianity, and all its depth and riches are contained in the knowledge of the Son of God. It is not a matter of how many methods we know or how many doctrines we have or how much power we possess. It is a matter of how much we know God's Son. If we know God's Son, we have the way, we have the truth, and we have the life. Our power comes from our knowledge of the Son of God. God has given us His Son, not many individual items apart from His Son. The crux of the matter lies in our knowledge of the Son of God. Let us now consider the meaning of "I am the way, the truth, and the life."

CHRIST IS THE WAY

"I am the way." A way can be considered as a method. The Lord meant that He is the way for us to go to the Father; He is the method by which we can go to the Father. If we have Him, we have the way. If we do not have Him, we do not have the way. If we have Him, we have the method. If we do not have Him, we do not have the method. Every true Christian has learned the lesson at least once that the Lord Jesus is the way; He is the method. If you are saved, you have gone to the Father through the Lord Jesus as your way. You at least have this experience. The Lord Jesus is the way, and no one can go to God except through Him. Every genuinely saved Christian knows that this is the only way that can be taken. Thank the Lord that many genuine Christians have at least learned one lesson, which is to go to God through His Son, Jesus of Nazareth. He is our way. We have taken this way at least once. This way is just Christ Himself; it is not a method apart from Christ. We need to see that not only do we have to come to God through the Lord Jesus when we are saved, but that the Lord Jesus is still the way any time we go to God; there is not some method outside of the Lord Jesus.

Some Christians are merely seeking for some methods to spirituality. Once a man was preaching on the subject of victory through Christ versus victory through ourselves. After his message, another brother shook his hand and said, "I have failed all these years. But today, everything is well." When the first brother asked why, he answered, "I have been seeking a method of victory. Thank the Lord. I have found the method! Victory is through Christ, not through ourselves!" The first brother told him bluntly, "If you have found a method, you will still fail." What does this mean? The Lord Jesus told us, "I am the way." In other words, the Lord Jesus is the method. A method is not something apart from the Lord Jesus. The method is the Lord Himself. If what we have is merely a method, it will not work. God has not given us a method; He has given us His own Son. We often hear of others' experience and admire it. But we do not realize that they have touched the Lord, while we have only seen a method. As a result, we fail again and again. The basic reason for this is that we do not realize that the Lord Jesus is the way.

We must remember that believing in the Lord and believing in a formula are two different things. Some Christians experience God's grace, and their eyes are opened. They see the kind of persons they are, and they drop themselves and believe in the Lord. They trust the Lord to do what they themselves cannot do. As a result they are satisfied in God, and they are liberated. A little while later, another person may come and, upon hearing the testimony of the first group, ask for God's enlightening also. He asks for God to show him his worthlessness, and he learns to trust in God, to be humble, and to deny himself. But strangely, the first group of people experiences deliverance, while the last man does not. One group is liberated, but the man is not. This happens because the first group of brothers have faith in God; they have touched the Lord. However, the last brother does not have faith; he is merely copying the formula of faith. He has not received God, but a formula of faith. In other words, the last brother has received a method from the first group of brothers; he has not received the Lord. There is no power in methods; methods will not work. They are dead because methods are things; they are not Christ Himself.

We have to remember that in spiritual matters, everything apart from Christ is death. Some brothers and sisters say, "It is so strange that when others have the faith, God answers their prayer. I believe just the same, but God has not answered my prayers. When others go to the Lord, the Lord is gracious to them. I do the same thing as they, but God does not grant the same grace to me." It seems as if they are putting the blame on God. They do not realize that they are believing in a thing; therefore, it is dead. A formula is worthless, and a method is useless. Only when we have Christ will everything be living. Even if you have learned all the methods, that will still not make you a Christian. God's children are produced by begetting; they are not produced by teaching.

The Lord Jesus said, "I am the way." Christ is the way; He is the method. Brothers and sisters, is your way Christ? Are your methods Christ? Or is your way just a way, and your method just a method? Praise the Lord. If your method is Christ, everything will work out. But if your method is only a method, even though it may truly be a good method or even the best and most correct method, it is still dead, and it has no spiritual value at all. Many prayers are not answered and many testimonies of believers have no effect on us because we have not touched the Lord; we have merely copied other peoples' methods. We have not touched the Lord ourselves.

Once a brother was preaching on Romans 6—8. After another brother heard it, he said: "Today I know the way to victory. I am clear. I believe that I will no longer fail as I did before." Another brother came up to the preaching one and shook his head. The preacher asked him what he meant, and he said, "I cannot say what the first brother said. The Lord has opened my eyes, but I dare not say that I have seen Him, and I dare not say that I have not seen Him." The second brother did not receive a method, but the Lord Himself. Eventually, he was able to stand. But the brother who thought that he would never fall eventually failed because he had merely gained a method; he did not gain the Lord. Therefore, it was worthless.

Many times, we are wrong even in the way that we listen to a message. We do not ask the Lord for revelation, and we do not ask to see the Lord. Instead, we exercise our mind to remember a method. Actually, even if we followed the method exactly, we would still not see any result. Sometimes, we may think that we have not seen very much; we may not be so confident as to say that we have seen the Lord. But in fact, we have seen Him. This seeing will bring about a real change in us. Thank the Lord that this is the way. We have not learned a method; rather, we know the Lord. The Lord shows us clearly that He is the method. Every time we hear a message or a testimony, we should ask ourselves, "Have I met the Lord, or have I merely understood a method?" The mere understanding of a method will not save us; only the knowledge of the Lord as our method will save us. A testimony by others of how they have trusted the Lord will not save us; only our own trust in the Lord will save us. The words may be the same in both cases, but the facts are vastly different. The Lord is the Lord of life. Those who touch Him touch life, and only those who touch Him will live.

CHRIST IS THE TRUTH

The Lord said that He is the way, and He also said that He is the truth. Truth is just Christ Himself. Truth is not words concerning Christ. Truth is not doctrines about Christ. Truth is just Christ Himself. Christians often consider expositions and explanations of Christ to be the truth. Actually, truth is not an exposition of a thing. Truth is just Christ Himself. The Lord said, "And you shall know the truth, and the truth shall set you free" (John 8:32). Brothers and sisters, let us consider how many truths have set us free. God's Word says that the truth shall set us free, that it shall liberate us. But many times, the truth is merely a doctrine to us; it is not Christ. Our eyes have not been opened to see Christ. What a pity that we have been preaching so many doctrines for ten years, yet we still have not seen. We may have heard many doctrines for ten years, yet we still have not seen. Men can speak about the doctrine of co-crucifixion, but others do not see the power of crucifixion in them. They can speak about the resurrection life, but others do not see the resurrection power in them. If what we preach are merely doctrines, then we only have things that are dead, not something that is living.

Once a person wrote a letter to a brother and said, "A brother has offended me. I do not know if I should forgive him. Therefore, I am writing to you. My heart is unbiased. If you say that I should forgive him, I will forgive him. If you say that I should not forgive him, I will not forgive him." Brothers and sisters, do you think that this sounds like a Christian? Suppose I have a loved one who has died, and I write a letter to others, saying, "My loved one has died.

Should I cry? If you say I should cry, I will cry. If you say I should not cry, I will not cry." If you heard this, you would surely laugh, because this is ridiculous. If one cries because others tell him to cry or does not cry because others tell him not to cry, his crying will be a performance, and his not crying will also be a performance. Both will be a performance, and both will be dead works without life. Here is a brother. You either forgive him or you do not forgive him. If you say, "I will forgive him if I know I should forgive him, and I will not forgive him if I know I should not forgive him," this is dead work based on dead teaching; it is even a kind of false performance.

Brothers and sisters, if we do not have the Lord living within us, and if it is not the Lord who is our truth, a teaching that guides our action is nothing but dead works; it is not life, and it is not living. Do you see the difference? The difference here is too great and too tremendous. Working requires that we exercise our memory, but life does not require us to exercise our memory. When we speak something out of life, we do not speak it because we remembered to speak it. A power within us motivates us to speak. The Lord is controlling us; a doctrine is not coaching or controlling us. The day will come when the Lord will open our eyes to see that spiritual reality is not apart from Christ. We do not present some doctrines to others. Rather, we lead others to Christ Himself. We do not need to remember a doctrine and then act according to it. Rather, Christ is living in us, and Christ is becoming our truth.

Once a brother offended another brother. The offended one could not contain himself, and he gave the other brother a severe scolding. After the scolding, his conscience bothered him, and he felt that he should go and apologize. Yet when he considered how the other brother had offended him, he could not help being angry again. Nevertheless, he felt that he had to apologize. So he prepared a letter to the other brother. The first thing he said in his letter was, "It was wrong for me to scold you." But he again recalled how the other brother was wrong to offend him, and he became angry again. After a while, he picked up the pen to start writing again. But while he was writing, he could not stop the hate and anger toward the other brother. After he finished the letter, he was still angry when he sent it out. Outwardly, it seemed as though the letter was a very proper Christian letter. But this was merely the result of teachings; it was not the result of life. Although he had written his letter and had apologized, he was still angry at heart. When he saw the other brother, he might be able to greet him and might be able to shake hands with him, but inwardly he had not forgiven him, and his speaking would not be natural at all. Brothers and sisters, do you see the difference here? The Lord is the truth. If what we do is a teaching and not the Lord, it is dead. We should realize that spiritual things are living only when the Lord is there, and they are dead when the Lord is not there. When the Lord shines within us, when He becomes the One working within us, and when we realize this inwardly, what we have will be living.

CHRIST IS THE LIFE

The Lord said that He is the way and the truth. Then He said that He is the life. We have mentioned briefly what it is for Christ to be the way and the truth. Now we have to speak some concerning Christ being our life. Wherever there is life, spontaneously there are works. But works cannot replace life. We have to be very clear that works are not life. Life does not require any effort of our own. Life is just Christ Himself. Many people try hard and exert considerable energy to be a Christian. Daily they strive toward this goal to the point of exhaustion. To them, the doctrines are strict; one has to be humble, meek, loving, forgiving, and enduring. These teachings are truly tiresome. They consider it a hard thing to be a Christian. This is especially true for young Christians, who find that the harder they try, the harder it is for them to live like a Christian. Brothers and sisters, if Christ is not the life, we surely have to do everything. But if Christ is the life, we do not have to do anything. Let me repeat: life is Christ Himself, and works cannot replace life.

Among God's children, the greatest misunderstanding is to think that self-effort is life and that unless one exerts his own effort, he does not have life. But we have to realize that if there is life, there is no need of work. If there is life, everything will be lived out spontaneously. Consider how your eyes see. Consider how your ears hear. Your eyes see spontaneously, and your ears hear spontaneously because they all have life. Life is so spontaneous. We must be clear that where life is, spontaneously there are works. However, works cannot replace life. Some works on the contrary prove the absence of life, or they prove that the life is weak. If it is life, it will surely result in good moral behavior. But good moral behavior cannot take the place of life. Suppose a brother is very gentle; he does not speak much, and he is neither too soft nor too hard. Some brothers may say, "This brother has quite a good life." But these brothers have actually used the wrong words. The Lord said, "I am the life." Although the brother may be gentle and quiet, his behavior is not life unless it issues from Christ. You can only say that he has a good temper. You can only say that he does not cause much trouble, or that he treats others politely, that he does not argue or quarrel. But you cannot say that this man has a good life. You cannot say that what he has issues from Christ, because what he has is natural; it is not life, and it is not Christ.

Some people hold to another concept. They think that life is power, and the Lord being their life means that the Lord gives them power to make them do good, behave well, and be a good Christian. They think that this is life. But God has shown us that power is not a thing. Our power is Christ; it is a person. Our power is not a drive to accomplish something; our power is a person. Our life is not only a power, but a person. It is Christ manifesting Himself from us, not us utilizing Christ to manifest the goodness that we desire to have. These two things are absolutely different, and we must distinguish between them clearly.

One brother went to meet in a place, and an elderly Christian asked him, "Why did you go to that place to meet?" The brother answered, "Because that place has life." The elderly man asked, "Is our place not as noisy as the other place?" The brother responded, "No, it is not noisy at all." The elderly man said, "What do you mean? If it is not noisy, how can it have life?" The brother answered, "It is not at all exciting, yet it has life. Life is not excitement; it is not emotional stimulation. Life is not a warm atmosphere or loud noise." The elderly man said, "Perhaps young people like excitement, but my preference is for thoughtful messages. Whenever I hear a thoughtful message, I touch life. To me this is life." The young brother replied, "I have also heard the kind of thoughtful messages that you speak of. But I did not touch life." Brothers and sisters, this conversation shows us that life is not emotional stimulations, good thoughts, wise words, clever words, logical words, or thoughtful words. All these may not be life.

Some may say, "This is strange. If life is not excitement and it is not thoughtful messages, what is life? What do you consider as life?" We admit that we cannot describe life with any better words. We can only say that there is something deeper than feelings and deeper than thoughts. When we touch this something, we become enlivened. This something is life. Brothers and sisters, what is life? Life is something deeper than the thoughts; thoughts cannot be compared with life. What is life? Life is something deeper than feelings; feelings cannot be compared to life. Thoughts and feelings are outward things. What then is life? The Lord said, "I am ... the life." One does not meet life when he walks into some excited atmosphere or some spiritually charged environment. We have to ask what is the source of such an atmosphere. Experience tells us that many people who are very good at creating a noisy atmosphere know very little about the Lord. Many excitable people know very little about the Lord. Christ is life; nothing else is life.

We have to learn to know life. Life is not a matter of excitement or thoughtful ideas. Life is an expression of the Lord Himself. We have to know the Lord. Nothing can be compared to our knowledge of the Lord. Whenever we know the Lord, we touch life. We have to realize before the Lord what it means for Christ to be life. Those who are excitable or who are smart are not necessarily the ones who know the Lord. But when there is a group of people who know the Lord in a particular way, who know what the Lord is like, their spiritual discernment of the Lord and their knowledge of the Lord will tell them that Christ is life. If we have such discernment and knowledge, we will be changed. If we know that the Lord is life, we will realize that in spiritual matters, natural energy is useless. If we know the Lord as life, we will look to Him alone. When we first believed in the Lord, we did not know what it meant to look to Him. But after we have learned some lessons, we begin to look to Him more and more, because we know that everything depends on Christ and not on us. When we first became Christians, we were after individual things, and we did not trust in the Lord. After we learned some lessons, we began to understand a little and began to realize that we have to learn to trust in the Lord. Trusting in the Lord does not mean trusting in Him for individual things, but trusting in Him to do what we cannot do in ourselves. When we first became Christians, we felt that we had to do something, and that unless we did something, things would fall apart, and everything would collapse. We always tried to do everything by ourselves. But after we find out that Christ is our life, we realize that everything depends on Christ and not on our working. Then we learn to rest and to look to Him alone.

Brothers and sisters, we must remember that God does not give us individual things, one by one. He has given us His Son. We should always lift up our head and say to the Lord, "You are my way; You are my truth; You are my life. Lord, I have to deal with You alone, not with the things that belong to You." Brothers and sisters, may the Lord be gracious to us and show us that spiritual matters are nothing but the Lord, that spiritual matters are nothing but Christ. Day by day, we have to realize that it is wrong for the way to be something that is apart from Christ. It is wrong for the truth to be something that is apart from Christ, and it is wrong for the life to be something that is apart from Christ. Yet how easy it is for us to take the way, the truth, and the life as separate things. We call a noisy atmosphere life. We call clear logic life. We call rich emotions life. We call outward behavior life. Actually, they are not life at all. We have to know that the Lord is the life. Christ is our life. It is the

Lord who lives out this life from us. May the Lord deliver us from many fragmentary, outward matters so that we can touch the Lord Himself. May we see the Lord in everything, and may we see that our way is our knowledge of the Lord, our truth is our knowledge of the Lord, and our life is our knowledge of the Lord. May the Lord open our eyes, and may we be delivered from many outward things to see the Son of God. May we live in Him, and may He live in us. Amen!

CHAPTER TWO

CHRIST IS THE RESURRECTION
AND THE LIFE

Scripture Reading: John 11:25

WHAT HE DOES VERSUS WHAT HE IS

Chapter eleven of the Gospel of John shows us how the Lord Jesus gave life to a dead person; it shows us how the Lord Jesus resurrected a person from among the dead. The Lord can resurrect man, but He did not say, "I will resurrect the dead." Instead, He said, "I am the resurrection." After He said these words, He resurrected a man. Both Martha and Mary were there on that day. To them, it would have been better for the Lord Jesus to say, "It does not matter that your brother has died; I can resurrect him." We like to hear this kind of word. Our desire and hope is that God will do something for us. We often pray, hope, and wait before God for a word concerning what He will do for us. But the Lord does not want to show us what He will do; He wants to show us what He *is*. What He can do is based on what He is. Martha believed in the Lord's power. She said to Jesus, "Lord, if You had been here, my brother would not have died" (v. 21). Martha believed in God's power, and she also believed in the Lord Jesus' power, but she did not see that the Lord Himself is the resurrection and the life. We must see that everything God can do is included in what God *is*. The reason a man does not have God's power is that he does not know what God is. "He who comes forward to God must believe that He is and that He is a rewarder of those who diligently seek Him" (Heb. 11:6). All the power that God has is based upon what He "is."

In John 11:25 the Lord Jesus was not saying that He can preserve a man's life, but that He Himself is life. He was not telling us of His ability to resurrect men, but of the fact that He Himself is resurrection. May God open our eyes to see who the Lord is. We must see that in God's eyes, Christ is our everything. Once we have this kind of understanding, it is possible to have genuine growth in spiritual things. We must realize that in God's eyes, there is not any other object; the only object is Christ Himself! Whether or not we grow spiritually depends on whether we have truly touched spiritual reality. In other words, do we just know the individual things that God has done, or do we know God Himself?

John 11 does not say that the Lord Jesus resurrected Lazarus. Instead it says that the Lord Jesus was resurrection to Lazarus. Brothers and sisters, do you see the difference? The Lord was resurrection to Lazarus, and then Lazarus was resurrected. The Lord did not give resurrection as a thing to Lazarus; He became resurrection to Lazarus. In other words, what the Lord does is only the appearance; what He is is the reality of the matter. We are not saying that the Lord did not resurrect Lazarus. We are saying that Lazarus resurrected because the Lord was resurrection to him.

We must remember that everything that God does in Christ is done in this principle. When the Lord is something to me, that something comes into existence. First He "is," then He "has." Many Christians separate the Grace-giver from the grace given by God. One day we will find out that the Grace-giver is the very gift given by God. God has not given us many things; He has only given us the Lord Jesus Himself. All spiritual things and all of God's gifts are but Christ Himself. God does not give us something piece by piece. God has given us Christ Himself. One day God will open our eyes to see that everything is in Christ. How wonderful it will be if we see this.

In declaring who He is, the Lord said, "I am the resurrection and the life." He is the resurrection. This is why His delaying did not cause a problem in the resurrection of Lazarus. In raising up Lazarus, the Lord was trying to lead men to the knowledge of Himself. The resurrection of Lazarus was not the greatest thing; the greatest thing is to know that the Lord Jesus is the resurrection. Many people believe that the Lord Jesus is the Life-giver. But it is altogether different to believe that the Lord Himself is life. He is not only the Life-giver; He is also the life. He is the Life-giver, and He is the life which He gives. He is not only the Lord who resurrects; He is resurrection itself. Once you see this, you will see that everything in Christ is living. God has only given Christ to man. We hope that at least a little light will shine on us so that we can know that the Lord is everything and know Him as such a Lord. He is the Grace-giver, and He is also the grace given. Our Lord said, "I am the resurrection and the life." Resurrection and life encompass the whole Bible. It is wonderful to know the resurrection and the life. Let us now see what life is.

CHRIST IS THE LIFE

God placed the man whom He had created in the garden of Eden. There were two options before the man. One was to receive life, and the other was to die. If man ate of the fruit of the tree of the knowledge of good and evil, the result would be death. But if he ate of the fruit of the tree of life, he would receive life. The man created by God was good, but there was still one unresolved question—the question of life and death. In the garden of Eden man could think and act, but he did not have life. We are not saying that he was not alive. As far as his natural life was concerned, man was alive. Genesis 2:7 speaks of man being a living soul. Nevertheless, as far as the life represented by the tree of life was concerned, man did not yet have life. The life we are speaking of is this life represented by the tree of life. At the time of Genesis 2, although man was alive, he had no life. Man had sound thoughts and sound feelings (these two being the most important elements of man's soul), but he did not have the life represented by the tree of life. From this we see that life is deeper than feelings and thoughts.

In Christianity, there are counterfeits to everything. There is false repentance, false confession, false salvation, false zeal, false love, false spiritual works, and false spiritual gifts.

Everything can be counterfeited; even life can be counterfeited. Many Christians think that good feelings are life. They think that an exciting atmosphere and loud noises are life. If you ask them what life is, they will not separate life from feelings; they always mix the two together. They do not realize that life is deeper than feelings. Other Christians do not take feelings as life, yet they take mental activity as life. This means that if there are enough ideas in a message to invoke mental activity, enough words to stir up one's interest, and enough doctrines to inspire admiration, they think that this is life. But those who are experienced and who have learned some lessons tell us that life is deeper than feelings and mental activities. Neither is life a kind of activity. We cannot say that just because a person is lively, energetic, and active, he has life. These are merely activities; they are not life. They are merely the performing of some activities; they are not the living of a life. We are not saying that life does not express itself in mental activities, feelings, or actions. We are saying that life is not feelings, mental activities, or actions. The words that come out of one person's mouth may be life, while the same good words out of another person's mouth may only be nice ideas. One may just touch excitement in one person, while he may touch life in another person. Many brothers think that when they feel a certain way, they have life. But an experienced brother will tell you that this is not life. Many brothers think that when they have a certain idea, they have life. But an experienced brother will tell you that this is not life. Two brothers may understand and expound a scriptural passage in the same way, but the strange thing is that an experienced Christian will sense a difference. One has both the right thought and life, while the other merely has the right thought. It is true that one often can touch life and mental thoughts at the same time. But we must not presume to think that touching the mind is equivalent to touching life. These are two different things. Many people think that because two people speak the same thing, they are therefore the same. But this is not necessarily true. It is possible that in one person we have the mind, while in the other person we do not have the mind, but life. Life is much deeper than mental activity; it is something deeper than good ideas. The Lord said, "I am the life." Life is the Lord Himself. Life is not something other than Christ. If it is a thing, it is dead; it is not life. To many Christians, life is something they can produce out of themselves. But the Lord told us that He alone is the life.

We need the Lord's mercy before we can see something concerning this matter. We can identify something as mental activity, we can identify something as feelings, and we can identify something as works. But we cannot identify what is life; there is no word to describe life clearly. We can only ask the Lord to show us what life is. Brothers and sisters, one day when the Lord opens our eyes, we will know what life is, and spontaneously we will touch the Lord.

CHRIST IS THE RESURRECTION

Let us consider again what resurrection is. Whatever encounters death and still exists is resurrection. Resurrection is that which withstands death and endures death. After man ate the fruit of the tree of the knowledge of good and evil, death came in and man died. Those who enter the grave never come out again. Once they go in, they never return. In the whole universe, of all men, only one came out of death. This One is our Lord. The Lord said, "I am...the living One; and I became dead, and behold, I am living forever and ever" (Rev. 1:17-18). The Lord is the resurrected Lord. Resurrection is that which passes through death but is not imprisoned by death. In the Bible, the authority of death is described as a kind of imprisonment. To imprison someone is to confine him and not release him. Once man enters death, he cannot come out anymore. Death imprisons everyone who enters it. But death cannot imprison Him. This is the meaning of life, and this is the meaning of resurrection. Resurrection is the life that passes through death and rises above death. Our Lord Jesus is the life. He became dead and was in Hades. He was in the deepest place of death. But death could not imprison Him. Death was unable to detain or keep Him. He came out of death! When life passes through death and is not imprisoned by death, this is resurrection.

Resurrection means that a life bears the mark of death, yet still lives; it is living, yet it also bears the mark of death. This is what is meant by resurrection.

Many people ask why is it that after His resurrection in John 20, the Lord Jesus left the mark of the nails in His hands and the mark of the spear in His side for Thomas to touch (v. 27). We have to realize that this is what is meant by resurrection. The Lord Jesus was not showing Thomas one who had never been wounded and one who had never died; He wanted Thomas to see that He was wounded but now alive. He wanted Thomas to see that He had died but now lived. The Lord has the mark of death in His body, yet He is now living. This is what is meant by resurrection.

We can apply this principle to ourselves. There are many things in us that do not have the mark of death; they cannot be considered as resurrection. Resurrection must be something that has the mark of death and yet is still living. Do not think that as long as you have eloquence, cleverness, and talent, everything will be all right. It is possible for you to have eloquence without the mark of death. It is possible for you to have wisdom without the mark of death, and it is possible for you to have talent without the mark of death. Whether or not others see the mark of death in our eloquence, cleverness, and talent determines whether we have resurrection. A brother may be very competent, capable, and apparently lively. However, he is too self-confident and self-assured. He thinks that everything put in his hands will be handled well. There is no mark of death with this person; one does not see any mark of death in his competence. Although he is self-confident, self-trusting, self-assured, and very energetic, the mark of death cannot be found in him. This does not mean that a person who has passed through resurrection has no ability in himself. It merely means that with such a person, there is the mark of death. He can still do things, but he dares not trust in himself anymore, and he has lost all confidence. His own energy has been weakened. This is resurrection.

Paul wrote to the church in Corinth and said, "I was with you in weakness and in fear and in much trembling" (1 Cor.

2:3). This was spoken by a man who knew God. What a pity that among Christians, there are too many strong and self-confident ones! However, here is a man who said that he was "in weakness and in fear and in much trembling." His body bore the mark of death, the seal of death.

Therefore, resurrection can never be separated from the cross. The cross removes something from us. Many things that originate from the self will not rise again once they have passed through the cross; they are lost in death. Whatever remains after it has passed through death, and whatever has the mark of death and is still living is resurrection. Resurrection must be something that has passed through death and whatever has passed through death must have suffered deprivation and loss. Brothers and sisters, if you really see what resurrection is, you will see what the cross is. You will see the stripping power of the cross. If you really know what resurrection is, you will find many things removed from you as you pass through the cross. If you really know what resurrection is, you will become another person; many things will be stripped from you. Only those things that have life will resurrect. Without life there is no possibility of resurrection. Suppose we cut a piece of wood into small segments and bury them into the ground. After some time, they will decay and become worthless. However, if we cut down a branch from a tree and plant it in the ground, after some time, it will germinate. In one case the sticks become rotten. In the other case the branch germinates. Anything that is dead rots, and anything that has life resurrects after it passes through death. Hence, the Lord's resurrection was based upon His life. Because there is an incorruptible life in Him, death cannot imprison Him. Since there is something in Him which cannot die, death was cast away even while He was put into death. When we go through the cross experientially, many things will remain in death and not come out. Only the things which are of God will resurrect. When we touch the cross, we ourselves will be eliminated. The cross is a big minus; it subtracts many things.

Many brothers and sisters often ask, "How do I know whether I am dead or not? How do I know that the Lord has done something within me through the cross?" It is quite easy to answer this question. If the Lord has done something within, you should have lost many things. But if you have been the same since the day you were saved, and if you are still as full as you were before, the cross has not done anything within you. If the cross has truly done something within, you will find that a great elimination work has been done; you will find that the Lord has done a thorough cleanup job in you. The result of this elimination is that you can no longer do what you could do before, and you are no longer capable of the things you were once capable of. You are no longer sure of what you had such assurance of before. Where you were bold before, now you become fearful. This proves that the Lord has done something within you. If resurrection is within you, many things have been left behind in the grave, because these things could not pass the test of death. Nothing in Adam can live once it passes through death. Anything that belongs to resurrection belongs to the Lord's life, the life which has passed through death and which has come out of death. Some things are lost through death, but are given back to us by the Lord. This is like the cutting of a branch from a tree. The branch seems to be dead. But when it is planted in the ground, after a period of time, it grows up again. This is resurrection. When we speak of having the mark of death on our body, it does not mean that we cannot speak or move anymore. Instead, it means that when we speak and move, we will not be as loose and self-confident as before. If a man has been touched by the Lord and dealt with by the cross, he will be weak, fearful, and trembling. He will not say, "I will do it," "I can do it," or "I can make it." From that time on, he will still work, but he will be very fearful of God when he works. He will still walk, but his walk will be a walk after God just as Abraham walked step by step with God. You will see the mark of the cross on such a man. Such a man will have been penetrated and pierced by God. He will not be as whole as he was before. There will be the mark of death on his body. This is resurrection.

Today God communicates with man in resurrection. Yet this resurrection includes the cross. Therefore, nothing that we have can contact God without passing through death. Everything in the natural realm has to pass through death. If we are not in resurrection, God cannot fellowship with us. He cannot contact us except on the side of resurrection. Hence, we have to pass through death to enter into resurrection. The life we have received is the resurrected life, and whatever we have that has to do with God is in resurrection.

One problem frequently encountered in the spiritual realm is that man's service to God is often based on natural things. Seldom do we see his service based on things in resurrection. Many people are very enthusiastic, but few have an enthusiasm in resurrection, an enthusiasm that has passed through death and that is still alive. Much enthusiasm is the first enthusiasm, not the second enthusiasm. We can find many brothers who are diligent and capable, but their capability is the first capability, not the second capability; such capability has never passed through death. If we live before God by the things in the natural realm, we are not living in resurrection.

Some have asked what the Body of Christ is. The Body of Christ is none other than the place where His resurrection is testified. In other words, anything that is not in resurrection cannot share a part in the Body of Christ. The church is not the place where you bring one thing and I bring another thing. It is not the place where you contribute your cleverness and I contribute my ingenuity. The church is not the place where you contribute something natural and I contribute something natural. The church shuts out all natural things and accepts only the things that belong to resurrection. Whenever natural things come in, the church will no longer be the church. In the church we cannot have anything that does not belong to resurrection. Many brothers ask how the church can be one. We need to know that oneness can never come through man's ways. The oneness of the church can only be achieved when God's children know the cross and deal with the flesh and natural things. If a man does not know the cross, whatever way he tries is useless. If the church resorts to natural means and human ways, nothing will be achieved. The church cannot have the flesh, and the church cannot have anything natural. If the flesh and natural things are brought into the church, the church will no longer be the church. It is true that the church needs people who consecrate themselves and who are useful, but the mark of death must be there. When we are useful, and when we also have the mark of death on ourselves, we have resurrection. We need to see that not only has the Lord Himself resurrected, He wants a church in resurrection also.

In order to have such experiences, we must look to God to work in us. We may be very familiar with many doctrines. However, if the Lord does not give us a fundamental blow, we will remain the same. Sometimes we fall and suffer pain, but this pain lasts only a couple of days or a few months. However, if we are broken by God in a fundamental way, and if we are broken deeply enough, we will not suffer pain for a few days or a few months, but we will have a scar over our entire life. We will remain crippled in God's eyes the rest of our life, and the mark of the cross will always be with us. Paul saw the vision once on his journey. Many years later, he still testified, "I was not disobedient to the heavenly vision" (Acts 26:19). If some day the Lord has mercy on us and gives us a severe blow, our self will never rise again, and the scar will remain on us forever. We can touch the nail scars in the resurrected Lord's hands and the wounds in His side. Today scars will be found on those who know the Lord and who experience the Lord as their personal resurrection as well. These scars will not pass away, and these scars will strip them of all their boastings; they will not dare to be self-confident, self-assured, or boastful of their own strength. Once a person is knocked down by the Lord, he will never be able to rise again. We hope the mark of the cross will become more and more apparent on us. It cannot be a performance or a pretense. Performance and pretense are useless. Whatever we do by ourselves is easily forgotten after a short time. However, once we are put on the altar and killed by the knife, we will never be able to rise up again. If we experience a fundamental blow, we will see that we can do nothing, we are nothing, and we are finished. If there is the mark of death on us, that mark will be a proof that we know resurrection. Those who know the cross know resurrection. Resurrection is whatever remains after passing through the cross. Many things will never rise up again once they pass through the cross. They are gone forever. Resurrection is whatever can pass through the cross. Only these things have spiritual value. Many things are brought into the grave and stay in the grave; these things are dead. However, many things pass through the grave and are brought to the other side; they bear the mark of the cross, and they are the things of resurrection.

May the Lord grant us the true knowledge of Christ as our resurrection. May we not only know Christ as our life, but also know Christ as our resurrection. May the Lord eliminate the many things that belong to us. May the Lord not only grant us more life and more of the things which are of Him, but may He eliminate all that we should not have. Many times we still live by our natural life and have not been broken by God. We have not seen God's discipline and have not known the cross. May the Lord have mercy on us. May the natural things in us be eliminated more and more, and may the things of resurrection be expressed more and more. May life and resurrection be a fact and not an ideal to us. Whenever we stretch out our own hands, may the Lord show us that there is no resurrection, but only naturalness and the flesh. May He show us the flesh by the way of resurrection. If we do not see this, may the Lord have mercy on us and grant grace to us. Amen!

CHAPTER THREE

CHRIST IS THE BREAD OF LIFE
AND THE LIGHT OF LIFE

Scripture Reading: John 6:35; 8:12

We have already briefly seen that all the spiritual things and all spiritual matters are Christ. God gives us Christ to be our spiritual things and matters. This is the crucial point in the spiritual life. Is our experience merely an experience? Or is our experience Christ? Is our righteousness merely righteousness? Or is our righteousness Christ? Is our holiness merely holiness? Or is our holiness Christ? Is our redemption merely redemption? Or is our redemption Christ? We often speak of the way, but the way we speak of may not be Christ Himself. We often speak of the truth, but we do not realize that Christ Himself is the truth. We often speak of the life, but the life we speak of may not be Christ Himself. In other words, we have many things other than Christ. This is the biggest spiritual problem among God's children. We say with our mouth that Christ is the centrality of all things, but in our living we still keep many things other than Christ, as if these things could help us live our Christian life. We must turn this concept around. We must realize that God has no intention for us to keep so many so-called spiritual things other than Christ. Under God's sovereign arrangement, there are things and matters, but God's things and matters are just Christ. Christ is all spiritual things. He is our righteousness; He does not give us a righteousness apart from Himself. He is our holiness; He does not give us a power apart from Himself that enables us to be holy. He is our redemption; He does not give us a redemption apart from Himself. He is the way; He does not open a way for us apart from Himself. He is the truth; He does not present us a truth apart from Himself and then charge us to understand it. He is the life; He does not give us something called life apart from Himself. Brothers and sisters, the more we go on in God's way, the more we will discover that there is only one grace among all God's graces. There is only one gift among all God's gifts. The grace is Christ, and the gift is Christ. Thank God that He is showing us that Christ includes everything day by day. Formerly, we thought of the Lord as our Savior. Today we can say that He is not only our Savior, but our salvation as well. This is amazing, yet it is a fact. When we were first saved, we believed in the Lord Jesus as our Savior. Now we can say that the Lord Jesus is also our redemption and our salvation. More and more we discover that Christ is God's things and matters.

If we wrongly presume that what the Lord Jesus gives is different from the Lord Jesus Himself, and if we wrongly presume that grace and the One who gives grace are separate, these mistakes will cause us to suffer great spiritual damage. It will cut us off from the source of life. Therefore, we need to see more concerning Christ being our things and matters. In John 6:35 and 8:12, the Lord tells us that He is the bread of life and the light of life. Let us first see how He is the bread of life.

CHRIST IS THE BREAD OF LIFE

The Lord Jesus said, "I am the bread of life." He said this to those who looked for Him in Capernaum. They expected the Lord to give them food, and the Lord told them, "I am the bread of life." This means that He is not only the One who gives the bread of life, but He is the bread of life itself. The Giver and the gift are one, not two. Thank God, Christ is not only the Giver, but also the gift of God.

What is the significance of bread in the Bible? In the Bible bread means satisfaction. The Bible uses hunger to express man's dissatisfaction. In order to solve man's dissatisfaction, man must have bread. Whether or not God's children have the strength to go on depends upon whether they are satisfied within. Today if we feel satisfied within, we have strength. If we feel empty like a tire void of air, no one can drag us along. We cannot say that we do not have life, but we can be without strength. Satisfaction gives us strength. Satisfaction enables us to walk. Such an inexplicable satisfaction makes us feel well.

Let us see what the bread of God's children is. The Lord Jesus said, "I am the bread of life." The Lord Jesus gives life, and He also sustains life. Many Christians think that the bread is just an hour's prayer or an hour of reading the Bible; they do not realize that the bread is the Lord Jesus Himself. We do not mean that prayer or reading the Bible is useless, but we should remember that the Lord Jesus said, "I am the bread of life." This means that the bread of life is just Himself. Many times God's children are not satisfied because they do not realize that Christ is the bread of life. We often meet hungry people, those who are not satisfied with spiritual things. They are not satisfied with this, and they are not satisfied with that. Every day they are surrounded by dissatisfaction. We are not urging people to be proud or self-satisfied. Pride and self-satisfaction are one thing, but eating to the full and becoming satisfied is another. Some people have been dealt with by God; they live before God fearfully, and they are in weakness and trembling. They are not proud, yet they have touched the Lord and eaten to the full. They are satisfied before God, and this satisfaction is their power.

How then can we be filled? How can we be satisfied? We need to know that all satisfaction is related to Christ and all satisfaction is in life. Christ is the bread of life. Whenever we touch life in a real way, we are immediately satisfied. Whenever we offend life, we immediately feel inwardly collapsed. We need to mention some concrete examples to see how man can be satisfied.

Some brothers say, "I have been busily working for more than one year, running here and there. I have been so busy that my whole being is drained. I am hungry, and I hope to go some place for a spiritual retreat." But when we read John 4, we realize that there is something wrong with these words. The Lord Jesus Christ was wearied from His journey and sat by the well of Jacob. The disciples had gone into town to buy some food, which shows that the Lord was hungry. At the well He met a woman of Samaria. God's will was for the Lord to speak to her and save her, and the Lord did it accordingly. When the disciples came back with the food they had bought, they invited the Lord to eat, but the Lord said, "I have food to eat that you do not know about" (v. 32). The disciples thought that someone else had given Him something to eat. Therefore, in the following verses the Lord said to the disciples, "My food is to do the will of Him who sent Me and to finish His work" (v. 34).

From this we see that working should only make us full; working should not make us hungry. Spiritual work should make us full every time we engage in it. If we become hungry every time we work, there must be something wrong. If we feel weak or deflated after we have worked, or if we feel that we are collapsing, it shows that there must be something wrong with our work. If our work is not separated from God's will, and if our work is not according to ourselves, every time we work, we will not collapse, but we will increase in strength. Many times there is not an adequate preparation before the Lord, and we begin to work because there is a great need from outside or because of others' urging. When we work under such circumstances, something within us will collapse, and we will not have the strength. After we finish such a work, there is no strength left within us, because something has gone wrong between us and the Lord. The more we participate in any work outside of God's will, the more hungry we will become. In order for us to be satisfied, we must follow God's will.

We must realize that Christ is our bread; our bread is not spiritual retreats or scriptural doctrines. We do not work until we become empty, and then go away for a rest; this is not our bread. Christ is our bread. We do not preach until we run out of teachings to speak about, and then go and find some new doctrines; this is not our bread. Our bread is Christ. Whether or not we are busy, if we have a word and the strength within, every time we stand up to speak for Christ, not only will the listeners be filled, but we will be filled as well. This is the result of the Lord working in us and in our life. This is why we touch the Lord. Eventually, after we are done, we will not feel any emptiness. Instead, we will feel that we have eaten a big meal and are full. It is wrong if we think that satisfaction depends on resting, on listening to messages, or on spiritual retreats. Food comes when we allow the Lord to do what He wants to do in us. The Lord is within us. Let us touch His life, and we will be satisfied.

In spiritual matters, one is not fed when he is at ease; he is fed when he is busy. While we are busy, we are fed. In spiritual matters, when we walk in the Lord's will, the busier we are, the more we will eat. We will not collapse through our busy schedules, and we will not become empty through these activities. I believe many brothers and sisters can testify of this. Suppose you talk to a person today, yet God has not moved in that direction; He has not spoken in you. Even though you may speak enthusiastically, after five or ten minutes of this kind of speaking, you will feel that something is wrong within. You may try to change the direction of your conversation because you feel that you cannot go on. Finally, when you leave, you will feel empty inside. There is nothing wrong with your words; the words are right, the attitude is also right, and you have tried your best to help. But the strange thing is that the more you speak, the emptier you become, and the more you feel that something has collapsed inside. When you leave, you will feel as though you have committed a big sin. Sometimes you may see some outward results and may feel that you have done a good work. But when these feelings pass away, you feel just as empty and hungry within. Whenever you do something by yourself, no matter how successful you are outwardly, inwardly you will feel deflated. Brothers and sisters, have you ever had this kind of deflated feeling? If your work is not done before the Lord, and if you are not following the Lord fearfully but are walking by yourself, even if you have the best motive or intention, you will still feel deflated and depleted of any spiritual vigor. You will feel as though the more you work, the more meaningless things become, and the more emptiness there is. Under such circumstances, the more others speak of your success, the worse you will feel inside. The more others praise you and mention the help they have received from you, the more you will hate yourself. This shows that your work is not a kind of bread, because it does not satisfy you. Brothers and sisters, those who know the bread are the ones who have found satisfaction in the Lord. Only Christ is the bread of life; only Christ can satisfy you. You will feel hungry with any work you have done if the work does not bring you in touch with the Lord. If you touch the Lord, if you touch life, and if you touch spiritual reality, whether or not you are busy, you will be able to say, "Thank and praise God. I have the bread. The Lord is my bread." Brothers and sisters, have you seen this? This is absolutely not something outward. The question is not where you have gone, what you have done, what message you have spoken, or how long you have spent in spiritual devotions. The question is whether or not you have touched the Lord within. Whoever touches the Lord is satisfied.

Some brothers and sisters may say, "What should I do? The Lord has not called me to preach in any place or to work in any place. Those who give messages and work have the opportunity to be filled. But we are not professional preachers and workers. Are we going to go hungry?" Brothers and sisters, thank God we do not have to be hungry. We may be doing only the smallest things; we may speak only ten or twenty sentences to others, or may speak only ten or twenty minutes to others. But as long as it is something out of the Lord, and as long as we do these things according to the Lord's operation in us, we will feel relieved and satisfied after we have done them. It is the Lord who gives us a burden, and once we unload the burden, we feel satisfied and full within. Once we touch God, we are satisfied and fed. Therefore, brothers and sisters, the workers do not have the exclusive right to eat; everyone has the chance to eat. Every day we have the opportunity to eat, and every day we also have the opportunity to be satisfied. Christ is our bread. When we touch Him, we have bread.

Let me mention a deeper example. We often think that something is good or spiritual, but this thing is not the Lord's will. When we carry it out, we feel empty inside. We can only be satisfied when we follow the Lord. Once a brother saw another brother walking in a wrong way. More than once he felt the need to clearly point out to the brother that the way he was taking was not a way of building up, but a way of corruption. However, he wanted to be a gentle Christian. He thought the best way was for him to smile and speak a few sweet-sounding words to persuade the brother. But every time he spoke in such a way, he felt like a glass with a hole in the bottom—everything had leaked out. In man's eyes, he did quite well; he was gentle, and he did not try to hurt anyone. In man's eyes, he was successful. Yet he felt hungry and unsatisfied. After two or three months, he felt wrong and came to the Lord and prayed for light. He asked the Lord to point out where he had gone wrong. One day he said to the Lord, "Lord, I will do whatever You want me to do." The Lord listened to his prayer and showed him what he should do. Later the other brother came again, and this one rebuked him severely. According to his nature, whenever he said a severe word to others, he would suffer for a few days. But the strange thing was that this time, the more severely he spoke, the more he felt he was touching the Lord. He also did not have to make a confession, which he always did after he rebuked others. Instead, he could praise the Lord. After he rebuked the other brother, he felt as though he had taken a good meal. This does not mean that we can rebuke others as much as we please. It is wrong to rebuke someone according to our will. However, it means that when we do anything according to the Lord's will, we are filled within, and we become stronger than ever. This shows us a fact: the good that we can perform by ourselves is not our food. We may think that as long as we can be gentle, everything will be fine. But experience tells us that even if we act gently, it is only our outward man who is doing it. It is a performance by our outward man, and this cannot become our food. Only when the Lord moves in us and we move according to His will, can we receive food. Whenever we touch life, we have food, and whenever we touch the Lord, we have satisfaction.

CHRIST IS THE LIGHT OF LIFE

The Lord not only said that He is the bread of life, but He also said that He is the light of life. Food is for satisfaction, while light is for seeing. When one is satisfied, he has the strength, and when one sees, he can walk. We have seen how Christ is the bread of life. Now let us consider how Christ is the light of life.

First, we have to point out that the light of life is not the knowledge of the Bible. Everyone knows that as Christians, we should read the Bible properly. But if we read the Bible as a book of knowledge, a textbook of theology, we will merely gain knowledge. If we read the Bible this way, we may gain some doctrines from the Bible which are truly scriptural. Yet these are mere letters. At the time the Lord was born in Bethlehem, many priests and scribes could memorize the books of the prophets, but they did not know Christ. Today even though we have one book more than they, the New Testament, it is still possible for men to know only the letters of the Bible without knowing Christ. We are not saying that we should not read the Bible. But we need to realize that when we read the Bible, it is possible that we will gain only knowledge instead of knowing Christ. Many of the priests and scribes had only dead knowledge; they did not know the living Lord. Many people think that the light of life is just knowledge, doctrines, theology, or church dogmas. Some persons say that they have received some light, but the light they are speaking of is not necessarily the light of life. The light they are speaking of may only be interpretations of certain verses or certain teachings. At most they afford others a little more Bible knowledge. The light of life is not knowledge or anything other than the Lord Himself. The Lord said He Himself is the light of life. The light of life is the Lord Himself.

Brothers and sisters, many people can tell us from their experience that what they see in the light of life is often difficult to articulate. Interestingly, those who see it see it, yet they cannot say what they have actually seen. Once someone talked to a sister to find out if she was saved. He asked her a few questions. She answered, "When I was first saved, I did not know what it was, but I knew I was saved. If you believe that I am saved, I am saved, and if you do not believe that I am saved, I am still saved." What she said is true. She was indeed saved, but she could not explain how she was saved. She knew it, but she could not explain it. Therefore, when the light comes, we may not be able to tell others many doctrines; it may be two or three years later before we can utter some doctrines or teachings. This light is the Lord Himself. When we see the Lord, we see the light.

What difference then does it make to us whether or not we see the light? What change will there be if we see the light? The difference is very great. If we truly see the light, we will fall to the ground. The light not only enlightens us but also kills us. Before Paul received the shining, it was not easy to put him on the ground. But once he received the shining, he fell. Some people always want to be humble. They try hard to be humble; they act humble in the way they speak and the way they act. But this kind of humility is very exhausting; even others feel exhausted for them. It is like a small child lifting a big dictionary; the book may not be very heavy, but it is exhausting for him to carry it. It is not easy for a proud man to be humble. It is not easy for us to fall down from the throne of pride. But once the light of the Lord shines on us, we fall immediately. We cannot explain it, but as soon as the light shines, we fall.

Teachings cannot make a man fall. A person can hear eight or ten teachings, and may even be able to recite them clearly and reasonably, but he remains the same. A message which should bring one to tears, or which should touch one's carnal living and bring a man to his knees, can be turned into a subject of study, and a person may think that he has received something spiritual. When a doctrine becomes a thing, a teaching becomes a thing, and words become a thing, the result is death; it is not light. One brother was so happy after he heard the teachings of Romans 6 that he thought he had seen Romans 6. But after a few days, he and his wife fell into a big argument. The Romans 6 that he saw was a thing; it was letters from a book; it was not the light. If what he saw wa

light, he would not have been the same. He would fall down
in the light. Light is piercing; it can do what a man cannot do.
A teaching will not do it, the brothers and sisters will not be
able to help, and our own effort will not achieve it. But the
minute the light shines, everything is solved. We may say that
we are very stubborn, but once the light shines, we will
become soft. When John saw the light, he became as dead
(Rev. 1:16-17). When Daniel saw the light, he fell toward the
ground as dead (Dan. 10:5-9). No one can see the Lord's face
without falling down, and no one can see the Lord without
becoming as dead. It is difficult to make ourselves die or
to humble ourselves. But once the light shines, everything
follows. The Lord's light kills. Once a man receives the Lord's
light, he falls.

The Lord Jesus Himself is the light. Hence, when a man
meets the Lord, he sees. When a man meets the Lord, he falls
and becomes weak as though he were dead. With many people,
their old personality is stubborn and has never been broken. It
is useless for others to try to deal with their personality. It
is also useless for them to try to deal with it themselves.
However, once the Lord's light shines on them, they receive
sight and become broken men. Whenever a man sees the Lord,
he becomes weak. Whenever a man sees the Lord, he is broken
and cannot survive. This is the meaning of light. Brothers and
sisters, we must never substitute any other thing for the light.
What we usually speak of as light is not necessarily light
itself. Most things are mere teachings and so-called truth.
They do not have any spiritual value to us. Once a brother who
loved the Lord very much met a man who said to him, "I am
very glad because I found the doctrine of sin in Romans."
When the brother heard this he said, "Friend, did you only
find the doctrine of sin in Romans today? I think you should
have found the reality of sin in yourself long ago." Many people
are looking for doctrines, but they have not found the reality.
Doctrines are mere words, and they are death. They are not
light, they are not life, and they are not Christ.

When the light comes, the first thing it does is kill. We
should not think that light only gives us sight. On the
contrary, when the light comes, the first thing it does is to

take away our sight. The light makes us see, but that is a later result. At first the light makes us blind and makes us fall; afterwards, we see. Anything that cannot make us fall to the ground is not the light. Anything that cannot humble us is not the light. Paul saw the light and fell to the ground, and his eyes could see nothing for three days (Acts 9:8-9). When we first encounter light, we become confused. When a person in darkness first sees light, he cannot distinguish anything; everything seems confusing to him. Anyone who is self-assured and who thinks he knows everything needs God's mercy, because such a man has never seen the light. All that he knows are doctrines and knowledge. Once he sees the true light he will say, "Lord, what do I know? I know nothing." The greater the revelation, the blinder one becomes, and the more severe a blow one suffers. Light makes a person humble; it makes a person fall. Only after this will a person see. If we have never suffered any blow and never been humbled, and if we have never been confused and never felt that we knew nothing, we have never encountered any light, and we are still in darkness. May the Lord have mercy on us so that His light may take away our self-assurance and so that we will not be so confident that we are right, that we are not wrong, and that we know so much. May we say before the Lord, "Lord, You are the light. Now I know that what I saw before was nothing but things."

Light is not something abstract; it is something very concrete. The Lord Jesus is the light. When the Lord Jesus was among us, He was light among us, the very light walking among us. What a pity that to some Christians so many things are abstract. They hear this and that doctrine, but everything is abstract to them. They only know some abstract doctrines, but have not received any practical help.

One brother was studying in a parochial school when he was young. He went to church often and heard the teaching concerning salvation many times. Yet he had never met anyone who was saved, nor was he himself saved. One day he met a man preaching the gospel. When he heard the gospel the man preached, he was saved. He had not been saved earlier because he had heard only abstract doctrines. On that day, he met a genuinely saved person; he met something concrete, and he was saved.

One brother once related his experience of studying the Bible. He said, "I had heard many brothers and sisters speaking on sanctification, and I went to study the doctrine of sanctification. I found more than two hundred verses about holiness in the New Testament. I memorized them all and arranged them in proper order. Yet I still did not know what sanctification was; it was meaningless to me. Then one day I met an elderly sister who was a truly sanctified person. On that day my eyes were opened, and I saw what sanctification is. I met a person who was sanctification. The light was so bright that it hurt; when it came there was no way for me to escape. The light showed me the meaning of sanctification."

From these experiences we can see that light is something concrete, living, and effective. If you merely convey doctrines to others, the result will be merely doctrines in them. This is dead, and this is not the light of life. The light of life will shine in their lives and will shine out from them. We must remember that with the Lord Jesus, light is something concrete. With us, it is also something concrete. This light is a living person. When this light appears, it is something living in us also.

Brothers and sisters, why does it seem as if God's Word has lost its power in these days? Why does it appear so weak and abstract? The only reason is that there are too many doctrines! There is too much "truth" and too much knowledge of theology! We have to realize that only the living Lord can produce living persons. May the Lord truly have mercy on us to show us as the days go by that all things are dead and only the Lord is living. In Christianity even the nicest looking things, the sweetest sounding things, and the things men consider most spiritual are dead if they are outside of Christ. The Lord Himself should be everything in us. He Himself is everything. Only He is living. He is living in us, and when He is passed on to others, He will be living in them as well. May the Lord be merciful to us so that we will prostrate ourselves before Him. When we do this, we will know the Lord in a way d.fferent than we did before.

CHAPTER FOUR

CHRIST IS GOD'S MATTERS AND THINGS

Scripture Reading: John 1:29; 6:53; 8:12, 24, 28; 11:25; 14:6;
1 Cor. 1:30; Col. 3:4; 1 Tim. 1:1; Psa. 27:1

GOD'S GOAL AND MEANS—CHRIST

God's goal is Christ, and Christ is also God's means. God uses Christ as the means to reach the goal, which is Christ. We can know and see God's goal particularly from the books of Ephesians and Colossians. In this message we would like to consider God's goal from these two books. There is one difference between these two books: Ephesians shows us that according to the economy of the fullness of the times, God wants to head up all things in Christ, the things in the heavens and the things on the earth (1:10); Colossians shows us that God has not only made Christ to be Head over all things, but God has made Him all and in all (1:18; 3:11b). Colossians shows us that God's goal is Christ, and His means is also Christ. God's goal is for Christ to be Head over all things. In order to arrive at this, God must make Christ to be all. He must be all and, at the same time, He must be in all. Only then will all things be headed up, for if Christ is all and if Christ is in all, all things will be headed up spontaneously.

Please remember that in God's eyes, there are not many things. In God's eyes, there is only Christ. In God's eyes there is no matter and no thing; in God's eyes there is only Christ. What we ordinarily think of as matters and things do not exist in God's eyes. We may consider that there are many matters and things in this world. According to our worldly view, there are matters and there are things. But in God's eyes, Christ is everything. There is no matter, and there is no thing. Christ is all the matters, and Christ is all the things. When the day comes that Christ is in all matters and in all things, God's eternal purpose will be fulfilled.

I hope that you can see that Christ has headed up all things in Himself. This does not begin in the future when God's eternal purpose is fulfilled; it begins today through the church.

Tonight I will not go too deep; I will only touch this matter briefly. God has ordained that all matters and things will be headed up in Christ in the future. How can all things be headed up? God says that Christ is all things. He is all, and at the same time, He is in all. When this happens, we will only see Christ in the world; we will not see matters and things anymore, because all matters and all things will have passed away.

Today in the church, God is starting to show us that Christ is all matters and things. When the church sees this, it will begin to live in the realm of the spirit. If the eyes of the church are set only on matters and things, it has not seen Christ yet.

The matters I am referring to are not the matters of the world, and the things I am referring to are not the things of the world. The matters and things I am referring to are spiritual matters and things.

THE REVELATION OF THE GOSPEL OF JOHN

Christ Being the Things of God

I would like to point out a very interesting thing here. The Gospel of John is the deepest Gospel; it is also the last Gospel written. It is the last book written in the New Testament. Many Epistles and books were written before the Gospel of John was written. John wrote his Gospel last. He wrote many things which are not found in the other Gospels. At the end he said that our understanding of Christ should be the same as God's understanding of Christ.

What we see in this book is not God's requirement for a lamb, or His gift of the bread of life. What we see is not just God's provision of a way, a truth, or a life. It is not a matter of the Lord having the power to restore man's life; it is not a matter of resurrection. It is not a matter of the Lord Jesus being able to give light, restore sight, and lead those who follow Him out of darkness. In the whole Gospel, we see only one great fact. This fact is that *Christ is all things.* The Gospel of John says that He is the light of the world; it does not say that He gives us light. It says that He is the bread of life; it does not say that He gives the bread of life. It says that He is the way; it does not say that He can show us the way. It says that He is the truth; it does not say that He can teach us a truth. It says that He is the life; it does not say that He can give us life. After Lazarus died, the Lord did not tell Martha and Mary that He had the power to resurrect their brother. Rather, He said that He is the resurrection.

Please remember that the bread of life is a thing, light is a thing, the way is a thing, truth is a thing, and life, resurrection, and the lamb are all things. But in Christianity, we do not find individual things. In Christianity, there is only Christ! Christ is what it is all about.

Today we have to see one thing before the Lord. We have to realize that in our experience there are not many matters and things. In our experience, there is only Christ. He does not give us the light; He is our light. He does not lead us to a way; He is our way. He does not give us life; He is our life. He does not teach us to understand a truth; He is the truth. Brothers, do you see the difference? All that God has given us is Christ Himself.

One day I told a group of people a spiritual fact. As I was speaking, many eyes began to stare at me. I said, "Let me tell you one crucial fact: God's Christ is God's matters. God does not have matters; God only has Christ! He has not given us light; He has given us Christ. He has not given us food; He has given us Christ. He has not given us a way, a truth, and a life; He has given us Christ. God's Christ is all things. Apart from Christ, God does not have any thing."

WHAT PAUL KNEW

Christ Being Our Hope

I would like to point out that not only does the Lord Jesus'

own word testify to this, but Paul said the same thing. He
knew the Lord, and he showed us one very interesting thing.
He said to Timothy, "Christ Jesus our hope" (1 Tim. 1:1). I
like this word. Do you like it? He did not say that our hope is
in Christ Jesus. Rather, he said Christ Jesus is our hope. We
do not put our hope in Him, and we do not draw hope from
Him. Rather, Christ Jesus is our hope.

Christ Being Our Life

Again he said to the Colossians, "When Christ our life
is manifested..." (Col. 3:4). He did not say, "When Christ is
manifested." Rather, he said, "When Christ our life is manifested." He said that Christ is our life. A Christian does not
have many matters; a Christian only has Christ.

Christ Being Our Wisdom: Righteousness, Sanctification, Redemption

This is not all. In these messages, the one verse that we
emphasize more than any other verse is 1 Corinthians 1:30.
What does it say? It says, "But of Him you are in Christ Jesus,
who became wisdom to us from God: both righteousness and
sanctification and redemption." God has not given us
righteousness; He has given us Christ. Christ is our righteousness. God has not given us sanctification; He has given
us Christ. Christ is our sanctification. God has not given us
redemption; He has given us Christ. Christ is our redemption.
God has not given us wisdom; He has given us Christ. Christ
is our wisdom. This is why we say that the Christ of God is
the things of God. God's Christ is God's matters and things.
Apart from Christ, God does not have any matter or thing.

Christ Being Our Righteousness

If God were to say to us, "I have made the Lord Jesus the
Lord of righteousness; He is the One who justifies you," what
would you say? You would say "Yes, He has justified us." But
God has not asked the Lord Jesus to be the Justifier; He has
asked the Lord Jesus to be our righteousness. Is this good?
This is excellent. He is not the Justifier, but our righteousness. He is our righteousness.

Christ Being Our Sanctification

Paul did not say that the Lord Jesus has become "the One that sanctifies." Rather, he said that Christ is sanctification. The Lord Jesus is not sanctifying us; He Himself is becoming our sanctification. God has made the Lord Jesus our sanctification. Our sanctification is Christ. Our sanctification is not a thing; it is not an act or a behavior. Our sanctification is a person—Christ.

Christ Being Our Redemption

Again Paul did not say that the Lord is our Redeemer. He said that the Lord is our redemption. Is this not strange? First Corinthians 1:30 does not say that God has appointed the Lord Jesus to be a Redeemer. Rather, it says that the Lord Jesus is redemption.

Thank the Lord that our Redeemer is Christ, and our redemption is also Christ. The One who sanctifies is Christ, and our sanctification is also Christ. The One who justifies is Christ, and our righteousness is also Christ. The One who gives wisdom is Christ, and that wisdom is also Christ!

WHAT DAVID KNEW

Christ Being Our Salvation

If I stand here and say to you, "The Lord Jesus is our Savior," you will respond, "That is right. The Lord Jesus is our Savior." But Psalm 27:1 tells us that the Lord is our salvation. It shows us that the Lord is our salvation and not our Savior. It is a fact that the Lord is our Savior. But God showed David that the Lord is our salvation. The Lord is our Savior, but He is also our salvation; He is that very thing. The Lord Jesus is the things of God. He is God's matters and God's things. The Lord Jesus Himself is the very thing that God has given us.

I have no intention of remaining too long on the exposition of the Bible. I am merely laying a foundation. If you spend some time to consider God's Word, you will see that Christ is God's things. God has not only given Him to be our Savior and our Redeemer. He has not only given Him to be the Lord of sanctification and the Lord of righteousness. He has given us Christ to be our things. Righteousness is a thing, sanctification is a thing, and justification is a thing, or a matter. But Christ is these matters or things.

THERE BEING ONLY ONE PERSON IN THE CHRISTIANITY OF LIFE

You may ask, "Brother, why do you have to spend so much time on all this?" I must tell you that this is the very difference between a Christianity of life and a Christianity of behavior. There is a vast difference between these two kinds of ways. The gap between these two ways is very great. One is spiritual, and the other is not. One is of God, and the other is of man's mind. These are two entirely different things. If you study God's Word, you will find that there is only one person in His Word; there are not many things. There is only the person; there are not matters and things. There is only one person—the Lord Jesus. Other than this person, one cannot find any other matter or thing.

The biggest problem with God's children today is that the Christianity they know is a fragmented Christianity. One person receives a little grace. Another person receives a little gift. A third person picks up tongue-speaking, while a fourth person experiences some changes in his behavior. Some have love, some have endurance, and some have humility. You may consider this as Christianity. Indeed, this is the Christianity that man speaks of today. But actually, this is not Christianity. Christianity is just Christ. Christianity is not a gift; it is not Christ giving you something. Christianity is just Christ Himself. Can you tell the difference between the two? These are absolutely two different ways; they are two entirely different ways. Christianity is not Christ giving you something. Christianity is Christ giving Himself to you. The problem is that in today's Christianity, man thinks only in terms of Christ's gifts. When he was a sinner, Christ gave him grace and mercy. Now that he has become a Christian, Christ gives him endurance and Christ gives him humility and meekness. It seems as if Christ is giving him many things.

THERE BEING NO NON-PERSONIFIED
THINGS IN CHRISTIANITY

In God's eyes, what is important is not the gifts of Christ. In God's eyes, He has given us Christ Himself. God has not given us humility or endurance; He has given us the whole Christ. Christ is becoming our humility, and Christ is becoming our endurance and meekness. It is Christ, the living Lord. This is Christianity.

Please remember that there are no non-personified things in Christianity. We must never receive a merely non-personified thing. In Christianity, all things are personified, and that person is Christ. In other words, our endurance is not a thing; our endurance is a person. Our sanctification is not an experience; our sanctification is a person, something personified. Our justification is not an experience; our justification is a person. Our righteousness is not an act; our righteousness is a person. Our redemption and deliverance are not something that we receive at one time; our redemption and deliverance are a person. Our endurance, humility, meekness, love, etc., are the Lord Himself; they are not things. This is Christianity. Christ is everything to the saints today. There is no need to wait for that day to come.

Many people ask how we can say that Christ is all. If you know the Christianity of life, you will acknowledge that He is all. He does not give all, rather He is all. These are two entirely different things.

Why is it that God's children fail so much today? They fail because they have only received a gift before the Lord; they have not received Christ. They have received fragmentary things before the Lord; they have not received the Christ God has given them. They have received only matters and things; they have not received a person. I do not know how much you have seen before the Lord. But I can say that when this question is resolved, all questions are resolved.

When we were saved, many of us heard God's Word, which says that He so loved the world that He gave His only begotten Son, so that we will not perish, but will have eternal life. When we heard such a word, we felt that we needed to be saved, and we went to God and prayed, "Lord, You have loved me and given Yourself to me. Can You give salvation to me also? You have become my Savior. Can You give me salvation also?" How foolish we were! We felt that having a Savior was not enough and that we needed salvation also! Many people have done this. And what do we do in our gospel preaching? We say that God has given us the Savior, yet when we repent, we pray, "God, grant me Your salvation." However, God has only one Son, and this Son is salvation. When we have the Savior, we have salvation. Do we still have to ask for salvation? Only a foolish man would say, "God, You have given me a Savior. Now please give me salvation."

"I AM ..."

Today we are Christians, and we are saved; God has given Christ to us to be our life. But we constantly ask for one thing after another; we ask for one, two, three, ten, fifty, a hundred, ten thousand, a million, and ten million things. We think that these individual things are important. But God shows us that Christ is our everything.

This is why God's Word shows us that Christ's name is "I am." Perhaps I should not be speaking so much of this matter outside the Bible; we should consider more of what the Bible says about this.

Food

In the Gospel of John, the Lord said that He is the bread of life. We often ask God for food; we think that there is something called food. We are hungry, and we ask God, saying, "Please give us food." But it is so strange that those who ask for food never receive food. Those who ask for food are always hungry. Those who beg for food are the ones who are always hungry. I cannot say that I have been serving the Lord for many years. But I can at least say that I have been serving Him for some years. During these years, I have never met a person who asked for food who received it. You may say, "Does this mean that God's Word is wrong? Does not Luke 1:53 say that He will fill the hungry with good things?" I say, yes, it is true that the hungry ones will be filled with good things. But with what are the hungry ones filled? We have to realize that what fills us is not food, but Christ. We often feel hungry, and we have a need. We feel empty and believe that God has food. So we pray and hope to receive food. But we do not know how we can get the food. All we know is that we should contact the Lord, believe more, receive more, and enjoy more. But the amazing thing is that when we believe more, receive more, and look to Him more, we do not get the food that we hoped for, yet we are filled. We do not receive the food that we expected to receive. But through our looking to the Lord, and through contacting and receiving Him, we are filled. God's food is Christ. His food is not just food. God has no matters; His food is just Christ. The Chinese have an idiomatic expression "Chien-pien-yi-lu," which means "a thousand pages of the same thing." It is not a good thing to be all the same. But before the Lord, all the things of God are "a thousand pages of the same thing." No matter what we are seeking before the Lord, what He gives us is the same—Christ; He is "a thousand pages of the same thing." He is the One who meets our need; things do not meet our need.

Righteousness and Sanctification

Many times, I can praise and rejoice for one reason only: my righteousness is not my conduct; my righteousness is a person, who is the Lord Jesus. Because the Lord Jesus has become my righteousness, every time I mention my righteousness, I can say that not only do I have righteousness or justification, but I can speak to my Righteousness, praise my Righteousness, and give glory to my Righteousness. Is this not a wonderful word? You may wonder how one can give glory to his righteousness. Yes, I often give glory to my Righteousness, because my Righteousness is the Lord Jesus. My sanctification is not my work. When I praise my Sanctification, I am not praising my work. No, I hate my work. Yet I can say that I praise my Sanctification, because my sanctification is my Lord. These are two entirely different things. Can you see this? It is not things but the Lord.

GOD'S TEARING DOWN AND HIS BUILDING UP

We can find one fact in our spiritual experience. Some

people have been Christians for one, two, three, five, or even twenty or thirty years. The strange thing is that when they first became Christians, they were very patient. But the more they went on as Christians, the more they could not control their temper, and the worse they became. I remember many people telling me that at the beginning, they were very patient; they could forgive, they could pray, and they could suffer any treatment from others. Others could treat them any way they wanted in school, at home, and at work. But now, they could not tolerate the same things anymore. In the past, they could do everything; now they cannot do them anymore. Sometimes they managed to hold back their temper, but something within them wanted revenge. We have seen too many examples of this kind. I can tell you a thousand, even ten thousand, stories like this one. Many people can testify that once they were humble, but they cannot be humble anymore. Once they were patient, but they cannot be patient anymore. Once they were loving, but they cannot be loving anymore. Once they were meek, but they have become stubborn. Once they were zealous, but they have become cold. They cannot explain this.

Brothers, we have to remember that God must take away everything that we have. When we first believed in the Lord, we felt that we lacked love, and we asked God for love. To put it in simple language, God gave us a "dose" of love, or a "packet" of love, so that we could love. It was a thing to us. We may have received plenty of these things. But God cannot allow love to remain forever as a thing in us; He has to put Christ into us. Therefore, He removes that love. Many people had a bad temper before they believed in the Lord; their temper was quick. After they picked up patience, patience became a thing, a gift, a salvation, or a spare part to them. As long as they had such a thing, they could work. During the first, second, and third year, these things may have served well. However, by the fifth year, or even as early as the third year, the situation began to change; the things themselves were gone. Today God is doing the same work in many of His children; He is removing all the things. Not only will He remove the worldly things; He will remove the spiritual things as well. Before you were saved, the matters and things of the world took the place of Christ. After you were saved, spiritual matters and things took the place of Christ. One day, God will show you that "Christ is all the world to you." Once God took away the things and matters of the world from you. Now he is taking away spiritual things and matters from you. He will take away your patience, your love, your power, your meekness, your humility, and everything that you have. He will show you that you do not live by patience but by a person. You will be patient because you have received a person, not because you have received a power. You will be humble, not because you have received a power, but because you have received a person. All the spiritual things have to go away. All the "its" have to go away.

For this reason, God's tearing down work, as well as His building work, goes on daily in many of His children. Daily "things" are torn down, and Christ is built up. This is the way God deals with His children. In the past, God might have given you a thing; He might have given you a power for endurance. You were so sure of this experience that you could almost write down the words: "My problem with endurance is over." Next you had to deal with humility, and God gave you another thing; He gave you the strength to humble yourself, and you were able to say that the problem of humility was also settled. When another thing is not settled, you pray daily before the Lord to try to solve it. You are always busy solving this and that problem. You are always trying to deal with this and that question. You are always dealing with individual problems. Brothers, God will take away many "things" from you; He will only give you One; He will only give you a person. This One will be your humility, your endurance, your meekness, and your love. He is the One who is. When you have Him, you can truly say, "God, You are the I am." This is Christianity. God is continually tearing down and building up. He will continue this work until one day we can say that Christ is everything. One day the universe will confess that Christ is everything. But first God wants us to confess within ourselves that Christ is everything.

Forgive me for speaking something about myself. I care much for many people and bear much of the responsibility for their spiritual condition. When I met a brother who was wrong, I often tried to exhort him. But I could only say, "Brother, you are lacking in love. Next time, you have to love your brother." He may have succeeded in loving, and I may have felt great that I saw some result to my work. But actually, what he acquired was love and not Christ. Love to that brother was not a person but a thing, a behavior. This is a Christianity of behavior. It is human conduct; it is man who is working, seeking, hoping, praying, believing, receiving, gaining, and acquiring something called love. This is why I say that love is only a thing and a behavior to him. But if that love is Christ, it is a totally different story. Christ alone is everything; it is not him. Christ is loving; it is not him who is loving. This makes love a law of life instead of an act of the will. This is a different kind of Christianity.

I do not know whether you have seen the difference. What do you feel when you render some help to a brother and open his eyes and help him to go on with the Lord? The most difficult thing we face today is that many people are merely involved in the things of Christianity; they do not know Christ and have not realized that God's thing is just Christ.

THE SECOND STAGE OF KNOWING

What does it mean to know Christ? I may say that knowing Christ is to know Him through matters and things. What does it mean to know Christ through matters and things? It means knowing that Christ is our matters and Christ is our things. Some people can say that they know Christ as their patience, Christ as their love, or Christ as their humility; this is knowing Christ. Once a person has this knowledge, he will have a thorough change. Once he has this change, he will say that his world does not consist of any thing anymore. I believe that some among us can say this, and some among us know what this means. In my world, my spiritual world, there are not many things. In my spiritual world, there is only Christ. I do not have any holiness; I only have Christ. But this does not mean that I am not holy; it means that

Christ has become my holiness. If you have this experience, you will immediately see that Christ is the One who is. This is the focus of everything—Christ is the One who is. If you have this experience, you will be delivered from all the outward things. The only question now is whether or not you know Christ. It is not a question of prayer, exhortation, or encouragement.

I wish to see my co-workers paying more attention to this matter. It is not a matter of exhortation or encouragement. If you try to encourage someone, at the most you will stir him up to do something by himself. But the only thing that counts is God opening man's eyes to know Christ. Even if I could repeat the things I have said a hundred times, it would still be useless. If God opens our eyes to see that Christ is the one thing we lack, everything is solved. Many people know Christ as the Lord of justification, but they still fear God and do not know that Christ is their righteousness. Many people know Christ as the Sanctifier, but they are still not sanctified. This is because they think that they lack sanctification. They think that the Lord is the One who sanctifies them, and they ask Him to give them the strength to become sanctified; they want to be sanctified. But while they are doing this, they find that they cannot make it. They cannot do it; they cannot be sanctified. Then God opens their eyes and gives them the light to see that Christ is their sanctification. God is not asking them to be sanctified; He is not giving them the strength to be sanctified. Rather, Christ becomes their sanctification. Christ in them has become their sanctification. When this happens, all problems will go away because He will be the "I am." I can afford to lose my power. But I cannot afford to lose Christ. My sanctification is not something I do in myself. My sanctification is something He has done in me. Once I know what Christ is to me, all the problems are solved. Christ is the One who is. I have nothing else to say. I have only one thing to tell you: Christ is the One who is.

The problem is that although many of us know that Christ is our Lord, we do not know that Christ is our matters and things. All those who know Him only as the Redeemer,

Justifier, Sanctifier, or any other "-er," only know His work;
they do not know what He is. But God wants us to know Him
as redemption, sanctification, and righteousness.

Let me ask a question: Is the Lord Jesus you know your
Savior or your salvation? Is the Lord you know your Redeemer
or your redemption? Is He your Liberator or your liberation?
Is He your Sanctifier or your sanctification? Is He your
Justifier or your righteousness. Those who know Him as the
"-er," only know Him in a superficial way. Those who know
Him as matters and things enter the second stage of their
knowing of Him, and their knowing of Him is higher and
deeper.

The problem among God's children is that there are too
many things. When we know the Lord as the One who is, our
things will become a person, and everything will be settled.
Then God's purpose, which He intends to fulfill in eternity,
will be fulfilled in us.

Whenever our holiness, redemption, regeneration, power,
grace, and gift only remain as things, we are barely touching
the periphery of Christianity. When we no longer see these
things as things, but as the Lord Himself, we will begin to
know God. Then we will begin to enter the goal of God's
eternal purpose. From that point on, we will no longer see the
many things of this world. We will see the Lord alone. He will
become the One upon whom all the issues hinge.

This is why I said at the beginning that many people have
things that are dead. Only when they understand what we are
speaking of here will their things become personified. It is
Him. Our regeneration is not a thing, but a person. We have a
personified One, not a thing. Everything that I have is personified, because everything that I have is the Lord. First, the
Lord leads us to know Him. Then He leads us to know that He
is our things. When we are led to know Him as all things, we
will be delivered from our own life, and we will be delivered
even from the spiritual world and spiritual things. From that
day on, we will truly say that the Lord is all and in all. We will
truly say that He is everything in our living. If I am patient
today, I am not the one who is patient, but Christ is my
patience within me. When I love today, I am not the one who is

trying to love. The power of love is not within me; rather, a person loves within me. If I can forgive today, it is not because I am forbearing, it is not because I have made any effort of my own, and it is not because I am capable. If I can forgive today, it is because there is One within me who is always forgiving. He is my forgiveness. We are humble not because we have told ourselves that we are too proud and that we have to be humble. We do not become humble by suppressing our pride or by making up our mind to be humble. Rather, a person is living out humility within us; He is our humility. This is why we can be humble. This is the law of life which we have been speaking of during the past few months. The law of life is nothing other than Christ becoming our things and Christ becoming our life.

Brothers and sisters, may the Lord open our eyes. We pray that He would truly open our eyes so that we would see. All things will eventually pass away, and only He will remain. Therefore, here in this place, we should only have Him alone.

CHAPTER FIVE

CHRIST ONLY—NOT MATTERS OR THINGS

Scripture Reading: John 8:28; Col. 3:3-4; 1:16-20

MAN'S THOUGHTS AND DEMANDS

The first gift we received from God was the Son of God, who is Christ. But different people have different degrees of knowledge of God. Among God's children, some know the Lord Jesus as one of the many gifts of God, while others know Him as God's unique gift. Many people confess that the Lord Jesus is God's gift, which means that they recognize Him as God's unique gift. But many other people accept the Lord Jesus only as their first gift. Apart from the Lord Jesus, they still see many other gifts. There is the first gift, but there are also the second, the third, the fourth, the fifth, the tenth, the thousandth, and even the ten thousandth gift.

When many people believe in the Lord, they accept Him and they are saved. But after they are saved, they find that in spite of their salvation, they still have many shortcomings and needs.

Some people find that they have a quick temper. Although they are saved, they still have their temper. Some people find that they are very proud. Although they are saved, their pride still follows them. Many people find that they are weak and timid. Although they are saved, they are still timid.

Hence, among God's children, we very often find that after many believe in the Lord Jesus and are saved, they hope, ask, believe, and pray before the Lord, and subsequently receive many gifts. They regard the Lord Jesus as one of the many gifts. They consider the Lord Jesus as one from among many gifts of God; that is, He is only the first among many gifts.

It is very interesting that at the beginning of our pursuit of the Lord we see many needs in ourselves. We think that since we are Christians, we should not do this and that. We are very sure that we are genuine Christians, yet we still have many shortcomings. It does not matter what the shortcomings are; as long as there are shortcomings, we consider them as wrong, and we try all we can to deal with these shortcomings. For this reason, we pray before God, we hope, we believe, and we strive, and eventually we receive something. When this happens, it seems as though we have overcome our shortcomings, and we rejoice in our heart that we have acquired a gift.

In this circumstance, many of God's children begin to think that the purpose of God's gifts and grace is just to fill up our lack. When some people hear this, they may ask, "If God's grace is not here to fill up our lack, what is it for?" Many people think that God's grace is for filling up our lack. This is like a Bible that has two thousand pages. If it is short one page, we try to make up the missing page. This is what we do when we try to use God's grace to fill up our lack. In other words, we think that we are lacking just a part; we think that we are lacking only a little and that as long as we can fill up that little part, we will be perfect. Some have said that they lack five things, and as soon as they have the five things, they will be satisfied. Some have said that they lack ten things, and as long as they have the ten things, they will be satisfied. Some may say that they have love and that they only need a little more humility, a little more patience, or a few other things. As soon as they have these few things, they say that everything will be fine. Man's thought is merely one of lack and shortage. What does he do? He prays to God and asks God to give him what he lacks.

But the problem is that many of us have come to realize that what we think we lack before the Lord and what we ask for are merely things. Our lack and our prayers are all centered around the matters and the things; they are all individual, countable objects. We say that we lack this or that, and if God will fill up our lack, everything will be all right. We lack patience. But what kind of patience are we looking for? Most of the time our eyes do not look to heaven. If our eyes did look to heaven, we would be looking upward. But most of the time, we cannot look upward; we can only watch and look at what is around us. We sigh and say that certain people are good but that we are not like them. What they have is patience, and what we have is a temper. What they have is meekness, but what we have is pride. We wish that we could be as patient and meek as they. Once I prayed to the Lord—it might have been my first prayer—that God would give me a Bible like the one I saw in a certain brother's hand. We can only pray for things that we see. We can only pray after we have seen something, and we can only pray for what others already have. We cannot pray for something from heaven which we have never seen. As a consequence, when we pray, we ask for patience like that of a certain person, or we ask for humility like that of another person. In our mind, we already have a picture of what humility is and what patience is.

If, when we were first saved, God had told us that He was going to pluck patience from a certain person and give it to us, would we not have been overjoyed? If we could have patience and humility on top of what we already had, we would have been satisfied and thought that we were perfect.

Patience is a thing to us; it is a thing that others possess. There is a certain thing called patience among the brothers and sisters, and we want it. We often hate ourselves, and we blame our parents for begetting us and giving us such a bad temper. We wish that we could be like certain persons, because they have something which we do not have. Many of God's children are after patience as a thing. They want something that will stop them from losing their temper. They think they need something called patience. With many people, patience is a thing. God has this thing, and it is found in many places on earth, but they do not have it. They think they need this thing, patience, so that they can become a patient person.

Here lies the basic difference between genuine Christianity

and wrong Christianity. Many of God's children are looking for things which they think can be found everywhere except in themselves. They think that it is found in Mr. Chang, in Mr. Yu, in Mr. Hsu, or in this or that person, but not in them. They are pursuing after a thing that can be found on earth. This is Christianity in the mind of many. They are craving for and pursuing after things, and they have acquired things. Many people only acquire a thing; yet their heart rejoices and they thank the Lord because they have acquired it.

THERE BEING ONLY CHRIST IN THE SPIRITUAL WORLD

Many Christians have not seen that there are not many things in the spiritual world; there is only Christ. There is no patience in the spiritual world; there is only Christ. There is no humility, sanctification, or light in the spiritual world; there is only Christ. There are not many things in the spiritual world; only Christ exists.

The Lord has to do a fundamental work in us. This is what we need before the Lord. If you would not misunderstand me, I will say that we need a second salvation. In our first salvation, we saw that our need was Christ and not works. We saw that salvation was through Christ and not through work. Now we need another strong and thorough vision: we do not need things; we need Christ. We need to have an experience as thorough and strong as our first salvation, and we need to have as many things torn down as when we were first saved. When many people were first saved, many things were torn down, and they gained Christ. In the same way, many things need to be torn down in them today. The difference is that what was torn down the first time were sinful things, while the things that need to be torn down now are spiritual things. The first time their pride, jealousy, vainglory, temper, and other sins were torn down. Now their patience, humility, and so-called holiness need to be torn down. These things must be torn down before they will see that Christ is their life and that He is the One who is. This inward Christianity is absolutely different from the Christianity that man commonly believes in.

If you would not be offended, I would say an honest word

to you. In the past, many brothers and sisters have come to talk with me and have asked me many questions. I could only say to them, "You may think that you are better than many people, but I am afraid that you will be the same as you are tonight for the rest of your life. You have many things. You have a great deal of patience and humility. You are a very capable and nice person. You are loving, helpful, and forgiving. You are willing to do this and that. Humanly speaking, it is hard to find a Christian like you. But I must speak an honest word: you only have things. You have to realize that what is truly spiritual before the Lord are not things, but the Lord Jesus Christ. What you are, what you can do, or what you have does not matter; only Christ matters. The only thing that has any spiritual value is what Christ has accomplished in you." In the spiritual world, there are not many things; there is only Christ. Christ is the matters and things of God.

TOUCHING CHRIST BEING TOUCHING LIFE

Perhaps I can cover some practical experiences. Please excuse me for mentioning some of my personal experiences. During the past few days, a brother encountered an accident at home. Because of my responsibility, I should naturally have gone to visit him. By visiting him, I would be able to help him by expressing my personal concerns and also save myself a considerable amount of work later—we should either want to be a loving Christian or not want to be a Christian at all. But the strange thing is that when I resolved to visit the brother, I became colder and colder within while I was on the road. Nothing seemed to respond within me. I immediately knew that I was trying to perform an act of love. I was trying to perform an act of brotherly love, but as I was doing it, I touched death. It was the right thing to do. It was a good thing, but it was not Christ. I was doing it myself. After I did this, the result was an inward death. I touched death within, and I became cold. I touched an act; I did not touch life. This was an act of love, but I did not find the Lord in the act; I could only say that I was the one who loved. Every time we touch Christ instead of a work, we touch life.

But every time we touch a work, we will surely die. Any time we try to do something by ourselves, we will surely die. We have to see that Christianity is just Christ. The Christian life is just Christ. We should not pile a thousand good things together and call them the Christian life. Even if we put all the patience on earth, all the humility, and the myriads of good things together, we still could not make a Christian. If we put the myriads of things together, all we would see is a list of things; we would not see Christ.

A few years ago, my co-workers were always teasing me about "face-saving." I not only tried to save my own face, but others' faces as well. I do not like to expose others, and I do not like others to feel bad when they leave my house. I do not like to embarrass others by what I say. Before others feel any embarrassment, I become embarrassed for them already. I like being a gentle person, but when I try to be a good and gentle person before my brothers, something within often tells me that I am dead. I immediately become dead. There is no more life in me, and I touch death. The only reason for this is that gentleness is a thing; it is something that I have worked up. It is not Christ. This is why I immediately fall into death. I touch a corpse. I become weakened and powerless. Something within collapses and tells me that everything is lost.

The problem is that, in God's eyes, whenever we are involved with a thing, we find nothing but death in it. Once we just have a thing, we immediately touch death because what we have is not Christ. But if we touch Christ, we will immediately touch life because Christ is life.

ONLY THE TREE OF LIFE BEING LIVING

We often become convicted in our work. Those who serve the Lord want to serve Him more. It is a good and right thing to serve the Lord. Our service to the Lord often demands that we suffer, sacrifice ourselves, and expend our energy and our money. But the strange thing is that when we do these things, we often do not touch life. Instead, we touch death, we become weakened, and we feel that something is wrong inside. Something within us tells us that we are wrong. Why are we wrong? While we are serving the Lord, while we are working and planning to do this and that for the Lord, we become weakened, and something within strongly rebukes us. Many times, the rebuke we suffer through sin is not as severe as the rebuke we suffer through doing many good things.

Many people think that the Lord within only rebukes them when they sin. But no! The Lord often rebukes us while we are doing good. The proper principle in God's eyes is not the principle of the tree of the knowledge of good and evil, but the principle of the tree of life. Being able to differentiate between good and evil is not enough. Everything hinges on life. All those who eat the fruit of the tree of the knowledge of good and evil will surely die the day they eat it; only the tree of life is living.

TWO KINDS OF CHRISTIAN LIFE

Among God's children, there are two kinds of Christian life. One kind is filled with things, and the other kind is just Christ. Outwardly, both kinds look equally good. One cannot detect much of a difference between the two. One talks about humility; the other also talks about humility. One talks about meekness, and the other also talks about meekness. One talks about love, and the other also talks about love. One talks about forgiveness, and the other also talks about forgiveness. Outwardly, both are more or less the same. They appear to be the same. But with one, we just have a list of things, while with the other, we have Christ. In reality, the two are entirely different.

WITH CHRIST, THERE BEING THE NEED OF THE CROSS

I would like to point out that when we have things, we do not need the cross anymore. With Christ, there is the need of the cross. The cross restricts us not only from sin, but from our own activity as well. The cross not only tells us that we should not sin, but forbids us from our own activities. The problem with God's children is that they think everything is fine as long as they do something well. They have not seen that the good things are only things. God cares for Christ. Christ is the very good thing. He is the life. If He does not move, we cannot move. It is easy for us to say many comforting words to others. But if He has not said them, we should not, because once we do, we will touch death; we will be inwardly weakened and deflated, and we will collapse. We can help others in many ways. We can be very gentle, and others may consider us nice men. But when we act this way, something within us collapses, and we become weakened. Here we see the need of the cross. The many things we gain through good works do not require the cross. When we allow the Lord to live in us to be our everything, and when He becomes our things, we need the cross. When He does not move, we cannot move. We have to ask the Lord to deliver us from good and righteous acts as much as we ask Him to deliver us from sins. It is easy for us to ask God to deliver us from sins, because we have condemned sins already. But it is not easy to be delivered from the natural life, because many of us have not condemned the natural life in us. We have not seen the natural life, and we have not rejected it.

CHRIST BEING THE HEALING

What does it mean for Christ to be our matters and things? What is the significance of having Christ as our matters and things? I think we can draw a good analogy from our physical body. Many people are very weak physically. They ask God to heal them. We find three kinds of results or three kinds of faith in this asking. Some people believe that God is their Healer. Others believe that God will give them health and heal them. But a third group believes that God is their healing.

How does a person pray when he has an illness? What does he seek after? He expects God to be his Healer. God is living, and he wants God to be his Healer, to touch him with His power, to be his Physician and demonstrate His healing power and healing ability. If this is the case, his God is as far from him as his doctor is from him. I wonder if you have heard what I said. This is a crucial word. Many people want God to be their Healer, but the distance between God and such people is as great as the distance between them and their earthly doctors.

Other people are a little bit better. They want God to heal them and give them health. Then one day God heals them, and they recover. Many people pray, make supplications, and expect healings. But why are they continually weak? There are still many weak ones among us today. Many people expect God to be their Healer or to heal them. But having God as the Healer and being healed are outward experiences; they are merely things.

What is the result of these experiences? Many times God is willing to heal us. I am not saying that God will not heal us. God can deal with little children this way. But many times, He will not deal with us this way. When we first believed in the Lord, God might have been willing to be our Healer, and He might have been willing to heal us. But after we have believed in Him for a while, He will put us in His hands, and He will educate us and teach us. Then God will no longer be our healer and will no longer heal us. God reserves the best for those whom He considers the best; He becomes healing to them. He does not give them healing, but *becomes healing to them*. He does not become the healing God to them; He becomes the living God who is healing to them. God is our healing. I do not know how to put this in any better way. I can only say this most reverently before the Lord, that Christ is our healing.

The trouble is that many people only see healing as a thing. They think that this is something apart from Christ and that everything is over after He has performed the healing. You may remember the story of the woman who touched Christ and how He felt the power go out from Him. The Bible says that He perceived that power had gone out from Him (Luke 8:46). I take the liberty to make this word more plain by saying that Christ Himself went out. He was not performing a healing. Rather, He was the healing. When He became the healing, men were healed.

We often may be weak and may still have physical ailments. But we can lift up our head and say to the Lord, "Lord, I do not expect You to be my Healer, only to go away after my sickness is gone. I do not expect You to heal me, and then find You gone even though the healing remains.

Lord, I expect You to be my healing. It is true that You are my Healer, but I want You to be the Healer in me. It is true that You are my healing, but I want my healing to be something personified. My healing should be a person; it should be something personified. It is a person who becomes my health." God becomes my health. Christ becomes my health. Is there a difference between being healed and knowing Christ as my healing? The difference is great! When I learned this lesson, I found that I not only possessed something called healing, but I possessed a person who has become life to my body. Once I saw this, all problems were solved, and I saw that my body has much to do with the Lord. When I have a problem with the Lord, my body immediately has a problem with Him. If He wants to put us through His test or do anything else to us, there is nothing that we can do to resist Him. Everything that we have depends on the Lord. We can only look to Him; we can do nothing. This is absolutely different from making healing a thing.

I thank the Lord for healing me many times. I can say that I was sick on a certain day of a certain month of a certain year, and God healed me on a certain day of a certain month of a certain year. I can tell you many stories about how I was healed at a certain hour of a certain day in a certain month and a certain year. I can count many cases of healing. But those healings were small healings. They were isolated things, and they can be counted. Whether there is one case, two cases, ten cases, or twenty cases, they can be counted. But I can also tell you another story, that at a certain hour of a certain day in a certain month and certain year, God opened my eyes to see that Christ is my healing. This is something that cannot be repeated; it is something that cannot be quantified. Once is enough. It is not a thing that can be counted. It is a person, a personified healing. My healing is a person who is in me as my healing all the time. Praise the Lord that this is a fact. Having God heal me and having Him as my healing are two entirely different things. One is a thing; the other is a person.

Paul was not healed, but he received the healing. Can we

see the difference between these two? Paul showed in
2 Corinthians 12 that he was not healed (v. 9). He did not
receive the thing which we call healing. But with Paul, we
see One who was his healing continually. His weakness
remained with him, but his healing also remained with him.
His weakness was chronic, but his healing was abiding. What
is a healing? To us, a healing is the removal of something. No,
healing is not a removal; healing is acquiring something.
Healing is not the removal of weakness but the presence of
strength.

When I first saw this matter, the light came very slowly
because my mind was filled with things; everything around
me was a thing. I did not realize that the Lord wanted to be
my thing, and I did not know that healing was not a thing. I
only knew that the Lord promised me something; I did not
know that the Lord wanted to be my healing. I only knew
about the Lord's promise; I did not know about the Lord as
my healing. One day I read Paul's story in 2 Corinthians. It
was very strange to me. It would have been an easy thing for
the Lord to grant him the healing. Removing the thorn was as
easy for the Lord as a doctor removing germs. But why did
the Lord not heal Paul? I prayed about this, and while I was
praying, the Lord showed me one thing. In 1923 Brother
Weigh invited me to preach at a certain place. In order to get
there, I had to take a little boat along the Min River. The
boats often became stuck to the riverbed because the water
was too shallow and the rocks were big. The boat owner often
had to tug the boat along. While I was praying, this scene
suddenly appeared in my mind. I said, "God, it would be easy
for You to remove the rocks. Would it not be wonderful if
You removed the rocks, and the boat floated on the water
instead?" I read 2 Corinthians 12 and realized that this was
exactly how Paul prayed. The water was too shallow, and the
rocks were exposed conspicuously; Paul prayed that God
would remove the rocks so that he could sail on the water
once again. But God answered by saying that He would not
remove the rocks. Instead, He caused the water level to rise.
When the water rises, the boat can pass over the rocks. This
is what God is doing. Our problem and our prayer are that

we are only for a thing—healing. But His answer is for Him to be our healing. When He is present, we can glide over our problems. Paul's weakness was still there; he did not use his own strength to fight it. If he fought with his own strength, he could only say that his own strength had tabernacled over him. But it was the power of Christ which tabernacled over him (v. 9). It was God who was working. There is a basic difference here. One is God giving me a thing, and the other is God Himself becoming my thing. God in me becomes the thing that I need. God Himself is that very thing.

"THINGS" CANNOT GO ON FOREVER

The same is true with spiritual things. What do many people desire and seek after? They are after a "thing." Many sisters have come to me and said that they want patience. I often felt that the word "patience" was too small to them. They wished they could be patient. They thought it would be wonderful if God gave them a dosage of patience and they took it and became patient. They sought patience. This is a dosage to them, and it will last for three to five days. But there is an expiration date on it. After a while, the word "patience" becomes smaller and smaller, until one day the word runs out. If it is a thing, there is always a day when it will run out. Even if it is something one receives through prayer, it will still run out. Sometimes to answer His children's immediate need and to accommodate their foolishness, God answers their prayers. But God does not answer such prayers all the time. He will not go on this way forever.

In God's world, there are not many "things." Christ is all and in all. God only has Christ. He cannot allow patience, humility, or love to continue to exist as things by themselves on this earth forever. What does He want in the end? In the end He wants to show us that Christ is patience, Christ is humility, and Christ is love. He gives Christ, not "things." One day when our relationship with the Lord becomes proper, the matter of patience will be settled. It is a matter of Christ, not a matter of patience. Once our relationship with Christ is normalized to the degree that God expects it to be,

CHRIST ONLY—NOT MATTERS OR THINGS 71

the matter of patience will be settled, the matter of pride will be settled, and ten thousand other matters will also be settled. The issue is Christ; the issue is not "things."

THE KNOWING OF CHRIST

Hence, in God's eyes everything depends on how we know Christ. What does it mean to know Christ? Some people know Christ as their love. Others know Christ as their humility. Some know Christ more, while others know Him less. Whatever "thing" you know Christ to be, that "thing" becomes your proper knowledge of Christ. This is the meaning of knowing Christ. The "knowledge of Christ" is not an abstract term; it is not something objective. Our knowing of Christ is positive and substantial. We know Christ by knowing Him as the various "things"; we know that He is this to us or that He is that to us.

Some of you can stand up and testify, "I did not know what it was to be clean, because everything with me, from my heart to my head and thoughts, was all unclean. But thank the Lord that Christ has become my cleanliness. God has made Him cleanliness to me." You can see immediately that this "thing" is not something that you have; this "thing" is Christ. When Christ lives in you, He brings this "thing" along with Him. It is something that He brings along with Him; it is not something that you have in yourself. This is genuine Christianity.

I must say bluntly that unless a child of God has his eyes opened to see that Christ is his things, he is not of much use, because all that he has is behavior. He is always the one who is doing the works. Even if he prays and God gives something to him, he only has temporary things that have no spiritual value in God's eyes at all.

To some people, grace from God comes in the form of separate individual things. To others, who also have the experience of grace, their grace comes in the form of a person, who is the Son of God. One day you will say to God, "I thank You and praise You because the grace I have received is Christ. My grace is a person; it is something personified." When you can tell the difference between these two things, you can tell the difference between life and death. Many brothers can only differentiate between right and wrong; they cannot differentiate between life and death. They can only differentiate between what is good and what is bad. There is only one simple explanation for this: they do not see that everything is in Christ. He, the person, is the matter. He, the person, is the thing. In the spiritual realm, there is only Christ; there are not many matters or things.

If God opens your eyes one day, you will see that this and that are things as soon as you touch them. This is very strange, yet it is very real. A man may be full of many things. He may be patient, meek, humble, faithful, loving, warm, forgiving, and merciful; he may be filled with many things. But what you see is only a big pile of things. You can at least tell the difference between a man's ring and his finger. You can at least tell the difference between a man's hat and his head, his glasses and his eyes, or his clothes and his body. If you can tell the difference between these things, you should be able to tell the difference between a thing and Christ. If you have never seen this, you will be surprised by what I am saying. But if you have seen this, you will see that this is a simple matter. Everything that is a thing is dead in itself, and outwardly it produces nothing but death. It is dead in itself, and when you perform this thing, if you have any spiritual sense at all, you will feel dead as well. While you are doing it outwardly, you sense that the result is death and not life.

The only thing you can say about certain persons is that they are very good, that they are nice men. You can only see good and evil in them; you cannot see anything spiritual in them. You can only say that some brothers are good, that they are nice men, that they have a good temper, that they are patient, and that they can suffer and deny themselves. That is all you can say. If patience, suffering, self-denial, humility, and love are only things, you may love them, but the minute you touch them, you are deadened within, and something collapses within you. There is a reaction against these things. Life has a strong reacting power. Sometimes a person says a very nice word, yet it is something that should not have been said, and there is immediately a very violent reaction within you against it. Take the prayer meeting as an example. What does it mean for you to say amen? It means that you are touched by life. When a brother prays, and the prayer touches your life, spontaneously you respond with an amen from within. Other prayers may be very earnest; the words may be very nice and the tone very loud, yet the more the prayer goes on, the colder you feel within. You wish that the prayer would stop because the prayer is exactly like the person who prays. There may be a thing, but it brings nothing but death. Just as a thing is dead in you, it is also dead in others. Things have no spiritual value at all, because man is doing all the work.

If what we have said is true, there is nothing more we can do before the Lord. We can only look to Him; we cannot do anything or perform any work. Brothers and sisters, we should realize more and more that works are abominable in the eyes of God. If we are truly led by the Lord to go on in this way, we will surely find out one thing: God hates sin, and He also hates behavior. When man sins, God says he will perish. When man behaves, God says he cannot be saved. God rejects behavior as much as He rejects sins. God only accepts one thing: His Son Jesus Christ. Only what Christ has done in us counts. Thank God that it is Him and not us. It is not we who are humble, but He. It is not we who love, but He. He does not give us the power; He is our power.

Brothers and sisters, I do not know what to say. I hope that the newly saved ones would pay special attention to this matter. As soon as you are delivered from the spiritual things, you will touch the Lord. The sooner you are delivered, the better it will be. The more you procrastinate, the more you will not see. Those who have many things piled upon them cannot see easily. God will have to do a great deal of work in chastising you and putting you down before He can take many things away from you and before you will take Christ. Nevertheless, as you advance somewhat in your Christian life, God will take things away day by day so that He can give you Christ.

I hope that this day will come. One day all the things in

heaven and on earth will be headed up in Christ. One day God's Word will be fulfilled, and Christ will be all. Those who do not know that Christ is all today can never expect that Christ will be all. Today Christ is all my things already. He is already all things to me. God has given us His Son already. He has given us Himself. This is what He has given us. Today Christ has to be all in us. There must be no difference between Christ and things. Nothing can be considered a spiritual thing in itself. Only Christ is all. All things are Christ. Christ is all and in all. This has to start in the church; it has to start with us today. We can declare that He is all because we know and acknowledge that He is all. We can also declare that He is in all. He is in our patience, He is in our meekness, and He is in our love because He is in all. One day (and we hope that that day will quickly come) God's Son will be all and will head up all things because He is all and in all! In that day, we will know that what we learned today is for that day. May the Lord bless all of us!

PRAYER

O Lord, we pray for grace before You. Lord, we confess that our eyes are blind; we do not see clearly enough. We know about things, but we do not know Christ. Our Lord seems so far away from us. The things seem so real to us, while Christ does not seem real to us. Lord, we pray that You would open our eyes so that Christ would become real to us, so that the things will pass away and life will fill us. Lord, we pray for deliverance from the many things, so that we can know the Lord as a person. May the Lord who is our person become our things so that everything in us becomes living and full of life, and so that others would see Christ when they see the things. Lord, we know that these two ways are entirely different. How different is the sinner's way from the way of the righteous. In the same manner, how different is the way of a genuine Christian from that of a false Christian. Many things need to be broken. You have to break us. Do not allow us to deceive ourselves, to think that we have seen it when we have not seen it, to think that we have touched the right way when we really have not touched it, to think that we are full of life when we are full of behavior, and to think that we are full of Christ when we are full of things. Lord, touch us. Lord, build up Yourself in us in a powerful way so that everything within and without us is just Christ, just Yourself.

Lord, bless these words so that they would bear fruit and would bring men back to Yourself in a rich way. May You utter what man cannot utter. May You cover man's weakness and forgive man's foolishness. May You gain something among us. We need to be laid bare. May tonight be the night when many are laid bare, when they see themselves as You see them. May a little light enter us, and may it shine through all falsehood and all performance so that we would see the replacements and everything that is not You. Bless Your own word, and glorify Your name. In the name of the Lord Jesus, amen.